Lessons 101

C. Heath Johnson

Also by Heath Johnson:

Dufus Monroe
Angels, Ghosts, and Desert Thunder
Holy Fire
Jellybeans

Copyright © 2013 C. Heath Johnson

All rights reserved.

ISBN: 10: 1490914560
ISBN-13: 978-1490914565

The stories in this book are true and derive from the author's personal experiences. Names, characters, and places have been changed where necessary to protect the identities and privacies of the individuals involved. Any resemblance to actual events, locales, or persons, living or dead, is a result of the author's faulty memory.

Life Lessons 101

To Mom and The Old Man:
both gone but not forgotten.

LESSON 1

Real Men Play With Dolls

This is a confession. Promise you'll keep this strictly between us.

When I was seven years old my mother, father, brother and I lived in a red brick, M-shaped apartment complex in Baltimore, Maryland. The red brick had blackened over the years shaded by the hard, polluted air of coal-burning factories and power plants nearby, as well as decades of city traffic- buses, cars, trucks, motorcycles, and every moving machines of the Twentieth Century. Deep wide shrubs with sharp stubby leaves- what my grandmother used to call "burglar bushes" -lined the building along the sides, and in front the low windows peeked out over flaring, waxy-leaved evergreens that my friends and I jumped in and treated as bouncy recliners. I used to get a horrible rash from the branches, but I didn't care.

Across the street was a series of narrow row houses that reminded me of cemetery crypts, with their dark stone porticos and narrow, gabled roofs, each door and window secured with wrought iron bars. Up the street along the shaded curve was a public golf course. It was nothing special, just a rolling obstacle course with patches of dirt and yellow grass down the fairways and small irregularly shaped putting greens. My father and a couple of his friends from the office played a round on the weekend now and then, but for us kids it was the perfect landscape for playing. Sometimes we would wind up in the line of fire when a foursome of cigar-chomping fat men in garish argyle pants and sloping golf hats teed off, but mostly they would wait until we moved. Occasionally one of them would lose his patience and wave his three wood in the air, questioning our parentage and threatening to come down and beat us like a bad habit, but most of the time the golfers managed to stay out of our way.

Golf. Who the heck cared about golf? Playing soldier was what mattered to us kids. Too bad if the hills and bunkers on the ninth green made a better battlefield than anyplace else around. There was nothing like the full-blown adrenaline rush of war: dodging incoming crabapple mortar rounds, tossing rock hard dirt clod grenades, running for cover across an open pocket of fairway amid a hail of rapid-fire acorns, or slithering out of a sand trap on your belly toward an unsuspecting enemy sniper and surprising him from behind.

"POW! You're dead!"

"Am not!"

"Are too!"

"Am not! You cheated!"

"Too bad, so sad. You're dead, Fred!"

Ah, yes, there was nothing quite like that glorious, stunned look in the other boy's eyes when he realized you had gotten the best of him, that you were close enough to drill a sleek, American-made .30 caliber pebble from your trusty M1A1 carbine slingshot right into his sternum. To a red-blooded American boy, nothing said manhood like a good old game of war on the ninth fairway!

Like most boys my age, playing soldier came naturally, like playing cowboys and Indians or cops and robbers. It's in every boy's genes: guns and shooting, getting the bad guy, enforcing the law and putting evildoers behind bars. Or better yet, on the gallows, or in the gas chamber, or, yeah! The 'lectric chair! Never mind the psychological damage or the disturbing symbolism of guns and rifles: the fact is, guys flash on the thrill of dropping something in its tracks.

The Krüger's lived next door to us in apartment 101 and were very nice people as I recall. They were the only family in the building my family knew, I guess because they had two children almost the same ages as my brother and me.

Jerome Holding and his sister Jessie, *my* only two friends in the entire complex, lived in the adjacent building on the first floor.

The Krügers would often have us over for dinner, and it was Mrs. Krüger who introduced my brother and me to French dressing on iceberg lettuce. For that reason alone we thought she was the best cook in the world. I can't recall a single other thing she ever served us, but by God, I remember her French dressing on iceberg lettuce. I also remember that the Krügers had a television, just like we did, but the difference was that when we ate dinner with them the TV stayed off. They were big into conversation.

Jessie Holding I remember for entirely different reasons. It was Jessie who led me, inadvertently perhaps, to the true portal of manhood. Her tomboy appearance may have had a subtle effect on me, and it may be that apart from jumping into the evergreen bushes with me and climbing to the top of the willow tree on the other end of the complex, and pushing me down the playground slide when I wasn't looking and knocking the wind out of me toughened me for the challenges of being a man in ways I might otherwise have missed. But more than boxing my ears, or hurling rocks at my head, or teaching me to cuss, Jessie trained me to be as rugged as a mountain by insisting I play Ken and Barbie with her in her apartment. Say what you will about scraped knees, chipped teeth, and bloody noses, playing Ken and Barbie with a girl who is ten times stronger than you are is how *real* men are made. It's boyhood boot camp. It didn't bother me that our tenuous friendship was always one click away from sudden death. Jessie made it clear from the beginning that if I didn't go along with her Ken and Barbie plans on any given day, she would not only beat me down to a whimpering pulp, she would also brand me as a sissy to every kid in Baltimore, the east coast, and the rest of the known world.

"All I gotta do is tell Millie Wadsworth," she said. "That loudmouth will have it on the six o'clock news before you sit down to dinner. 'Heath Johnson plays with dolls!'"

"You wouldn't dare."

"Try me."

That was Jessie's trump card: Millie Wadsworth. Always megamouth Millie Wadsworth. If I didn't play dolls with Jessie, she would tell Millie Wadsworth that I did anyway, so what chance did that give me? I would have no refuge and no hope of ever making another friend for the rest of my life. Apart from being invited- no, *forced* -to play Ken and Barbie with Jessie, playing with dolls actually became a not-so-bad pastime for me, especially on hot summer days, since we were inside and the Holdings were one of the lucky families that had a window air conditioning unit in the living room. The fact that that I got to drive Ken around in Barbie's turquoise Mercedes Benz convertible sports car didn't hurt and may have actually helped lay the solid emotional foundation I would need years later as a teenager. Thanks to Jessie, Barbie, and Ken, I entered puberty with confidence and unmatched bravery when it came to knowing my place in the social food chain and understanding girls and their quirky, unfathomable, girlish idiosyncrasies.

I'm not sure exactly how much harm was done to my mental and emotional wiring as a result of playing dolls with Jessie Holding, but I remember that after a while I started to enjoy dressing and undressing Barbie. I got a kick out of all the different outfits she got to wear, and I wondered why it was Barbie had such a huge variety of clothes and outfits and Ken had only a few choices. I mean, how much fun can you have dressing a thirteen-inch flesh-colored doll in a tux or a cotton sports shirt and slacks? The way Jessie and I played, Ken was always in a tuxedo anyway, picking Barbie up for a date. Still, putting him behind the wheel and driving him and Barbie all around Jessie's bedroom was fun, if only because it helped me picture what driving a real car on a real date someday would be like.

Little did I know at the time- and if I knew where Jessie was today I would thank her -that playing with Ken and Barbie also prepared me for Stage II of my training as a play soldier when, only a few years later, I graduated to G.I. Joe. By the time I reached the fifth grade, I was a recognized expert in military outfits and paraphernalia. Every boy in school knew me as the go-to guy when it came to outfitting G.I. Joe. I had all the gear, all the uniforms, all the accessories. From combat fatigues and dress uniforms, to Navy Seal scuba gear and parade-ready dress blues. I was the all-knowing G.I. Joe outfitter.

Remember, this was at a time when the Vietnam war was escalating and Americans watched Dan Rather in the trenches every night on the network news, reporting the action back to

Walter Cronkite in New York. "Uncle Walt" would then punctuate Dan's report with the day's official body count: "four Americans killed, twelve wounded, with fifty-six enemy soldiers killed." It made even a kid like me as proud of my country as I was of my Cub Scout uniform and all my merit badges. Our guys were running up the score against the North Vietnamese enemy just the way we overran the Birchfield kids on the ninth fairway.

What I could never figure out, though, was why the accompanying news footage always showedAmerican soldiers dragging dead and wounded G.I.s through the mud into waiting helicopters and looking panicked as they sprayed bullets wildly at the jungle, toward some unseen enemy out of the camera's view. I figured it was like the craziness of the war games on the golf course. Some days you were feeling it and you popped them in the sternum with pebbles until they finally surrendered, and other days you dove for the bunker and got pelted with acorns anyway. It was just that it seemed as though most nights our guys were diving for the bunkers and getting bombarded with crabapples and acorns.

Fortunately, though, my experiences with Ken and Barbie- and especially dressing Barbie in all her different outfit combinations -prepared me for the excitement of war and the realities of life. If it hand't been for all those days of mixing and matching outfits for Barbie and coming to understand that Ken was an expendable lunk, I would never have been ready for G.I. Joe and knowing how to outfit *him* for any situation in peacetime or combat. Because I knew all about G.I. Joe, I knew the answer when the old man downed the last of his martini, turned the TV in the dining room to the evening news, and asked, "What the *hell* are we doing in Vietnam? Will somebody please explain it to me?"

"Because that's what G.I. Joe does, Dad."

"That so?"

"Yeah."

"Eat your dinner."

Which I would . . . while my mother, father, brother and I watched American soldiers shoot their guns at the jungle and drag their buddies through rice fields to waiting helicopters.

LESSON 2

Taming a Lion

A broken bottle lying near the curb was all the temptation I needed.

I was seven years old, and I had no idea whose car I had sabotaged, or even if the tire would go flat after it ran over the beer bottle I'd strategically placed behind the right front wheel. The bottle was *supposed* to shatter and, I hoped, at least one shard would penetrate the tread, but these things are tricky. It was critical that Mr. Jacobson not see me set the trap.

His Buick was parked on the near side of the street in front of our apartment building, and Mr. Jacobson, who lived in the apartment above ours, hated kids and everybody knew it. He was the perfect target. He was a grouchy old man, retired, and he sat in his window to spy on us kids just to see if he could catch us doing something he didn't like. The day before he had yelled at Jessie, Jerome, and me for using colored chalk to draw on the sidewalk, and he had made Jessie cry- not an easy thing to do.

"Why can't we draw pitchers?" Jerome demanded when Mr. Jacobson wagged his gnarly pale finger in Jerome's face.

"It messes up the sidewalk, that's why!" Mr. Jacobson squeaked. "Makes the property look like a ghetto."

"It does not!" cried Jessie.

"It damn well does, you impudent little brat! Now get a hose and scrub this graffiti off before I call the police!"

Jessie was the toughest girl I knew, and I had never seen her so much as flinch, let alone tear up and cry. So when she ran home sobbing, I knew I had to avenge her. Mr. Jacobson went inside our building and climbed the stairs to his second floor apartment and slammed the door. Jerome and I could hear it all the way outside.

"He can't tell us not to draw pictures," I said defiantly, but Jerome had already started following his sister home. "See you tomorrow!" he called, and broke into a run to catch up with Jessie.

"Who does he think he is?" I asked no one out loud. "It's not *his* sidewalk." I couldn't believe Mr. Jacobson had broken up our game of picture drawing like that. He had a lot of gall bossing us kids around like that, telling us what we could and couldn't do. The sidewalk belonged to *everybody*, not just him, the old turd.

Get down out of that weeping willow before you break off all the branches! Don't go so high, you're going to break the whole swing set! Take your lemonade stand down to the corner! You look like street urchins begging for handouts! With Mr. Jacobson, it was always something.

I walked down to the corner, the one where the shady weeping willow stood, feeling dejected and angry, wondering why people like Mr. Jacobson had to be so mean to other people and how come he couldn't just leave us alone and let us play.

Then I saw it: a dirty, dark Schlitz beer bottle lying against the curb, crying out softly, *Pick me up. Take me with you.* So I did.

To anyone else it probably would have looked like just another beer bottle in the road, but to me it looked like an opportunity. I wasn't sure *what* opportunity, maybe just to hurl it across the street and watch it shatter against a tree trunk- you know, just to take out some of my frustration -but whatever was going to happen next, the bottle felt good in my hand: smooth and hard and . . . *glassy*. I walked back down the sidewalk toward our building, thinking. When I reached the short set of steps that cut into the hill in front of our apartments, inspiration struck. I saw Mr. Jacobson's unguarded Buick sitting there, asking to be vandalized. *You made Jessie cry, you bastard. Now you're gonna pay.*

I made my move. I checked up and down the street, glanced up at the front window of Mr. Jacobson's apartment to make sure he wasn't watching, checked our apartment to see if my mother might be watching, then quickly crouched to wedge the bottle just under the front tire of the car and run around to the little playground behind the building before anyone could spot me.

My improvised plan was foolproof. I would pretend to be playing on the monkey bars and swing set in the back courtyard, creating an alibi just in case Mr. Jacobson accused me of puncturing his tire, which he was bound to do, since he accused me and Jessie and Jerome of doing everything else wrong in the neighborhood. My mother would see me on the swing set through the kitchen window which faced the rear of the complex, and would swear to the police and anyone else who asked that she had seen me innocently playing in back on the monkey bars when the crime took place out *front*.

When enough time had gone by that I was sure Mom had seen me, I strolled around front and, just as pleased as I could be with myself for having plotted such clever revenge against old Crab Cakes Jacobson, took the stairs two at a time up to our apartment, and deliberately let the door slam behind me.

"Heath!"

"Sorry, Mom!"

I scrambled over to the front window and watched, giggling, for Mr. Jacobson to get in his car and run over the beer bottle. With any luck at all, his tire wouldn't go completely flat until he was blocks away I sat at the window for what seemed like an hour, but eventually I grew bored of staring at a parked car and moved to my old man's favorite gold wingback chair and thumbed through the latest issue of Life Magazine. My imagination absolutely tickled with glee as I pictured Jacobson sweating and cursing when he had to jack up his car and fix the flat.

My mother, in the meantime, was cooking dinner in the kitchen. It was almost six o'clock, and my father was due home from the office at any minute. I had to remain cool and calm, no matter how excited I was on the inside.

Mom called from the kitchen. "Heath, did you get that flat tire on your bicycle fixed yet?"

Momentarily caught in my reverie, I missed the word "bicycle" and panicked. All I heard were the words "flat tire."

"I didn't do it!" I cried.

"Well, you know, if you don't get that tire fixed your father isn't going to do it for you."

Oh, God, I thought. *She knows!*

My eyes enlarged and swiveled in their sockets. I suddenly had a very sick feeling in the pit of my stomach, a queasy sense that my mission was going to fail. Something told me she was onto me. I wanted to confess everything, to tell her right then and there what I had done. She would smooth everything over, she always did, and she would always have my crime to use against me later if she needed to.

Life Lessons 101

"I'll fix it," I pleaded, "I promise!"

Just then I heard a loud bang outside in the street. POW!

My heart skipped beat, my breath caught; the magazine fell off my lap. I looked outside and realized a passing truck had backfired.

"What's wrong with you?" Mom asked, standing in the doorway of the kitchen. She walked over and picked up the magazine. "That's my brand new copy of Life. If you're not going to take care of it then put it back on the rack and leave it alone, do you hear? And make sure you get that flat on your bike fixed before your father finds out you haven't taken care of it."

My breathing became regular again; I felt lightheaded but relieved. "Yes, Mom," I answered.

She didn't know!

"Heath, you're acting a little odd. Are you sure you're okay? You look pale."

"I'm okay. But you can take my temp-a-chur if you want."

"No, I don't need to take your temperature. Maybe *you* should go outside and play for a little while."

Outside! Are you out of your mind? I'll get caught for sure.

"Naw, I was just out there. There's nothin' to do."

"Well, then, why don't you go to your room and play with your soldiers for a little while? See what your brother's doing. Dinner won't be ready for another half hour, and Dad's going to want to have a drink before we eat when he gets home."

I cast a narrow glance at the window facing the street. "Can I watch some TV instead?"

"No TV. We'll watch the news at dinner. Why don't you read a book?"

"Yeah, okay." I went to my room to retrieve the Hardy Boys book I had started the night before and then sprawled out on the living room floor to read. But I couldn't concentrate; my conscience troubled me.

"Your brother's in his room playing," Mom called from the kitchen. "Why don't you go get him and read your book to him?"

"Do I have to?"

"He's your brother. He likes it when you read to him."

"No, he doesn't."

"Yes, he does. Now, go."

Reluctantly, I got up and walked back to David's room. "Mom says I should read to you," I told him.

"Go away."

"I can't. Mom wants me to read the Hardy Boys to you."

David pitched a fit. "My Lincoln Log house is almost done! Why do I have to listen to a dumb story?"

"It's the Hardy Boys, you ignoramus," I said. "It's not dumb."

David sprang up and dashed to the kitchen. "Mom, don't make him read to me. I'm workin' on something important."

"Heath's a wonderful reader, David. You should spend more time together."

"He hates my guts," said David.

"He doesn't hate your guts," Mom assured him as she poured a bag of frozen peas into a tortured, gray pan.

"Does too!"

"No, he doesn't. That's silly."

"Yes, I do!" I insisted. "I hate his guts! He ruins everything!"

"Do not!"

"Do too!"

"Do not!"

"Stop it! Both of you! I'm not going to stand here and listen to this bickering. Heath, you go outside. David, play with your Lincoln Logs. And don't let me hear another peep out of either one of you."

David went back to his room, lay on his belly and carefully placed another green slat across the roof of his Lincoln Logs "fort." Against my instincts and judgment, I headed for the front door to go outside, but just as I took hold of the doorknob, it rotated in my hand. Startled, I jumped back. In walked my old man, his dark suit smelling as it always did, musty with the odor of a full day's worth of Lucky Strike cigarettes. I looked up at him dumbly. "Hey, Number One Son," he said.

"Hi," I said.

"Dad!" David shouted, bounding from his room.

"Hey there, Punky! How's my boy?" He set down his briefcase and hoisted David toward the ceiling. David laughed and flapped his arms. "Hey! Look at me! I'm flying!" A sudden drop thrilled him even more, and he screamed with delight as the old man scooped him out of the air just before he hit the floor. Another hoist and drop had my brother running around the living room in positive delirium.

I watched the old man half sigh, half whistle, and rub his temples as he plopped himself into the gold chair. He loosened his tie and undid the top button of his shirt. "Come sit on my lap, Number One, and tell me. You been good today?"

"Un-huh," I mumbled.

"That's it, just 'un-huh'? Tell me what you did today."

Haltingly, I explained in needless detail everything, except one, I had done during the day. He listened patiently, and when I finished he ran his hand across my crew cut with approving strokes and said, "Sounds like you've been busy."

"Rough day, dear?" my mother asked. She brought a fresh-stirred martini out and kissed the old man on the cheek. "Better drink quickly. Dinner will be ready in a few minutes." That was my cue to slide off the old man's lap and take my rightful place on the couch. He lifted the glass to his lips and took a sip. Then he lit an unfiltered Lucky Strike.

"Yep, whatever you say," he said, blowing a plume of smoke into the room and running his hand across his own crew cut. "How long 'til dinner?"

"About ten minutes. The roast is simmering and I've got the peas and potatoes going now."

The old man took a long sip of his martini, and calling to Mom in the kitchen said, "Jack Wengaman called a meeting today about the Bangkok project."

"Oh?" Plates clattered in the kitchen.

"Yeah. He and Rune Gross flew in last night and it seems that-"

He was interrupted by a loud, confident knock at the door.

"Dear, would you get that?" Mom called. "I'm about to whip the potatoes."

"Yeah, okay." He gulped the last of his martini and retrieved the olive with his finger. David opened his mouth to receive it, but the olive went another way, toward me. The old man dropped the olive in my open mouth. "Thanks," I said.

David sat on the couch by me as the old man went to answer the door. When he opened it, I felt something vital get sucked out of me, as if all my guts had just been vacuumed out. I could hear Mr. Jacobson at the door, and I slithered to the end of the sofa just far enough to get a peek. Mr. Jacobson stood in the hallway, his graying carrot-colored hair tinted with green in the fluorescent lighting. His eyes were slits, glancing at my old man briefly before zeroing in on me. With a ferocious I-mean-business expression on his face, he spoke in a low, serious whisper, his lips thin and stretched. He held something in his hand, but I couldn't see what it was. Like a slowly developing summer storm, I saw the horizon darkening.

Whatever Mr. Jacobson was holding, he handed it to the old man. "All right, all right, Abe," I heard my father say. "No need to snap the strap on your toupee. I told you, I'll take care of it."

"I oughta call the police, that's what I oughta do!" I heard Mr. Jacobson say, because he raised his voice loudly enough for the whole first floor to hear.

My father closed the door and threw the deadbolt. Upstairs, I could hear Mr. Jacobson's door slam. The old man turned to me and held up a familiar-looking beer bottle.

"What's that?" David asked.

With only slits for eyes, the old man focused on me. "I'm not sure. Maybe Heath knows."

"Dear?" Mom broke in, "who was it?"

"Abe Jacobson."

"What did he want?"

The old man nodded authoritatively at me. "Well?"

Sand burrs suddenly stuck in every nerve of my body; I heard my mother's concertina voice behind me as I fixed my gaze on the evidence in the old man's hand. "Heath?" she said, "Did you do something with that bottle?"

I wanted to say yes, to be honest with the two people who had always been honest with me, but the beer bottle moved, and instantly I looked up into the old man's eyes. "I didn't do anything!" I protested. "I didn't do anything!"

Oh, my God. How did he know? How did Jacobson find out?

The old man's mouth curved downward like a scythe. "Mr. Jacobson says he saw you put this under the front tire of his car," he said.

I felt as though I had been electrocuted, high voltage shooting through my spine and out all four arms and legs. I didn't dare make my predicament worse by pleading I was the innocent victim of mistaken identity.

"Well?" the old man intoned, taking a step toward me.

Tears moistened the corners of my eyes, but the only sound I could make was a single, faint whimper. I slid my hands into the rear pockets of my pants, an instinctive act of self-preservation.

"Good thing for you Mr. Jacobson was looking out his front window and saw you place the bottle under his tire. If he had run over it he would have ruined a perfectly new Goodyear radial whitewall- which *I* would have had to pay for."

David's face, a study in sibling rivalry and vindication, appeared in my peripheral vision. He was only too happy to see me sitting on the hot seat again to care whether my impending punishment would leave him an only child or not. He dashed into his bedroom and pulled a pillow up by his open door in anticipation of watching my execution from a comfortable distance. I knew what was coming, and I couldn't think of anything to do except plead my case and hope the old man understood.

"He made Jessie cry!" I blurted.

"Who made her cry?" Mom wanted to know.

"Mr. Jacobson! He yells at us for everything. I was just gettin' him back."

My father set the dirty beer bottle on the coffee table, then towered over me, his hands on his hips. "So ruining one of Mr. Jacobson's tires was going to even the score, is that it? he asked.

"Wull, yeah. Sort of."

"Okay, let's go," he said.

I knew what *that* meant. "Let's go" was the signal that a severe whipping stood between me and dinner. It was the same as "Gentlemen start your engines!"

It was only a half-dozen steps to my bedroom, and I knew there was no talking the old man out of this one. Gently but firmly he took me by the elbow and guided me to the execution chamber. When we reached the doorway to my room he stopped, turned to David, who had followed us, and gave him "the eye."

"Go help your mother in the kitchen," he ordered.

"She doesn't like it when I help in the kitchen," he said.

"GO, boy!"

With that, David scurried back to his room instead and shut the door without another word.

When the old man and I were in my room, he shut the door gently. I had no reason to doubt that I was about to receive a harsher version of the bare bottom smack down than I had ever gotten before for trying to sabotage Mr. Jacobson's brand new tire. He took the orange tortoise shell hairbrush off of my dresser and tapped it lightly against the palm of his free hand, always an indication that the punishment about to be handed down was going to hurt me a lot more than it was going to hurt him, despite his claims to the contrary. Just the thought of him slapping that hairbrush on my naked rear end sent chills down my spine and produced an imaginary sting so real I could feel tendrils of fire shooting down the backs of my legs, clear to my heels. Without the old man even giving the order, I dropped my pants and briefs and squeezed my eyes shut, prepared for the bite of cold hard plastic on my unprotected ass. But there was no slap, no stinging smack. The shock I expected never came.

"Pull 'em up," he said.

Not sure what he had in mind, I did what he said, thankful to know that whatever punishment he had in mind was apparently not going to involve physical pain.

"Sit down," he said, inviting me to join him at the foot of my bed. "Look, son, I know Mr. Jacobson is a sourpuss and picks on you kids a lot. Hell, he gives the adults a hard time, too. Some people are just naturally cranky. But that doesn't mean you're entitled to unbridled revenge."

I had no idea what *unbridled* meant, but I knew enough to realize that the winds of change had shifted in my favor. Then it hit me: maybe the old man was toying with me, delaying the inevitable. He was going to talk first and tenderize my psyche. He planed to lull me into thinking no punishment was coming after all, and then, just when I believed a pardon had been granted, he would hurl me back across his lap and thrash me. I shut my eyes again and held my breath, bracing for the body throw and the whipping. I wished I had never *seen* that glass bottle!

Still, there was no grappling, no struggle, no spanking. A thousand years could have passed and I would not have understood what was *not* happening.

"Now listen to me," he said, "and listen to me good."

I nodded that I was listening.

"If you're going to get back at old man Jacobson- or anybody else -with a beer bottle for making your friend cry, you have *got* to break the bottle first. Have a jagged edge pointed up at the tread, ready to inflict damage. An intact bottle's just going to shatter and send pieces flying everywhere. It won't cut the tire. You understand?"

I looked at my dad with slack-jawed disbelief. This was my old man talking? *My* old man? Mr. Law and Order?

"I guess," I said.

"What do you mean you 'guess'? Either you comprende or you don't."

"I understand."

"Good. Now, you've already tried the beer bottle trick, so you're going to have to come up with something different, something less obvious. Got any ideas?"

I was still flummoxed at this unanticipated solidarity, so my mind was blank. "No," I said.

"No, *what*?"

"No, sir."

"That's better. Now, as soon as you come up with something, something that will teach that horse's ass to leave you and the other kids alone, and that won't cause death or personal injury, you can come eat dinner. Not before. Am I clear?"

I studied him as if he had cucumbers growing out of his nostrils. "Y- yes. Sir."

With that he patted me on the knee, then stood and left the room, closing the door behind him. I sat on the edge of my bed, stunned, guilt-ridden, wondering what kind of reckless, otherworldly stunt I could pull that he would approve of.

I focused on the poster hanging on the wall over my dresser. It was a Barnum and Bailey circus poster I had gotten in the spring when the circus came to town. It was a busy piece of art, really, a kaleidoscope of acrobatic, clownish and ferocious images revolving around a ring master, and the full-mane head of a roaring lion. To the left of the lion, a tamer in pith helmet and handlebar mustache held a pistol in one hand and a whip in the other. I wondered how a creature as ferocious and beautiful as a lion could be so controlled by the gestures of a single man. Was it the whip? The pistol? The shouted commands? It certainly wasn't intimidation. I blinked and thought about it. Why didn't the lion attack the trainer?

After many minutes of thought and reflection, I came up with a great prank and an answer. The prank was easy: it involved grease and some fishing line. The answer was not so easy. The reason the lion didn't tear the tamer to pieces, and the trainer didn't shoot the lion, I guessed, had something to do with their relationship. It might have been mutual respect or distance, but my hunch was that it was a little bit of both.

Just like me and my old man.

LESSON 3

Beachcombing For Answers

I was never a whiner when I was a kid; I was a *why-ner. Why do I have to do this? Why do we have to do that?* Used to drive my old man crazy. "You don't always *need* to know why," he'd say. "Sometimes you do it *because I said so.*"

This was not a lesson that registered with me right away.

By the time I was eight years old, my old man had walked the beaches of the East coast from Long Beach Island in New Jersey, to the rippling Outer Banks of North Carolina and every named and nameless stretch of sand in between. But it was the discovery of Smith Island, off the lower Eastern Shore of Virginia, that set him to dreaming of salt water fishing greatness.

It wasn't much of an island, really; it was a barren, windswept, storm-torn sand bar pocked with deep, sucking mud and salt marsh, not much more than an isolated strip of surf that was a haven for ocean surf anglers like my my old man and his best friend, Stretch Griffith. They were after lunker channel bass, but the island was a wonderland for a pair of eight-year-old kids like me and Stretch's son Skip. Crabbing barefoot in the slurping grey marshes, tracing the low dunes for pieces of grooved driftwood, beachcombing for conch shells and upturned horseshoe crabs, Skip and I discovered our own Never Never Land. Ignoring sunburn, sand fleas, and especially channel bass fishing, Skip and I would stroll the island for hours examining with barely contained excitement the skeletons of fishing trawlers that had run aground decades earlier and left, with their lock box treasures, petrified timbers protruding from the dunes like sad, weathered rib bones. Skip and I couldn't have cared less about fishing; exploring for treasure and wondering if the ghosts of pirates and the drowned crews of those doomed trawlers would reveal themselves after dark and haunt our campsite in the middle of the night.

  Stretch and my old man had first found the island on a calm October morning as they scooted in Chopper, Stretch's twelve-foot Starcraft boat, south on Magothy Bay, off the coast of Virginia. The moon was full, and at 3:30 a.m. my father looked out across the black, moon-splashed water, and as he did Stretch replied to the unasked question: "Yep," he said, "that's the place."

  As it turned out, though, the channel bass had already passed for the season. All the old man and Stretch hooked on that trip were some big sharks. They never saw a single channel bass.

  Several return trips to the island and a couple of fifty-pound channel bass catches later, convinced Stretch and my old man that they had found the perfect barrier island. They were careful to keep the secret to themselves, though, even when fellow anglers back on the mainland pressed them for tips about where they were finding these monster fish.

  One autumn, the old man and Stretch decided it was time to initiate Skip and me in the ways of beach camping and surf fishing. I was never sure exactly why my old man thought surf casting was a rite of passage I needed to experience, but I didn't care, either. A fishing trip with the old man meant a long weekend of adventure and at least two days away from school. Even though I had never gone with him before, I knew the routine: pack provisions the night before, load and check the tackle box, roll and tie off sleeping bags and tent, break down and stow the old man's 13-foot fishing pole, check life vests, sun screen and waders. It resembled a military operation, only without the organization.

I was sent to bed at 8:00, right after dinner, with orders to get as much sleep as I could; Mom would come up to wake me at about one a.m. I could never get to sleep, of course; I was too amped about the trip to sleep. Instead, I turned on the little transistor radio I kept hidden under my pillow and listened to the muffled sounds of Top 40 with Cousin Bruce on WABC in New York. I listened for a while, fantasizing I was one of the Beatles or the Rolling Stones. The next thing I knew, Mom flicked on the light by my bed and started gently shaking me.

"Come on, Mr. Fisherman, time to get up! You're burning moonlight!"

I rolled over and pulled the covers over my head. "Do I gotta get up now?" I muttered.

"Your father's already got the car packed. He's downstairs ready to go," Mom said.

That was when I realized that even though it seemed as though I had been wide awake listening to the radio all that time, I had actually drifted off to sleep. I pulled on a shirt, a pair of jeans and my sneakers, and with the aroma of strong black coffee wafting through the house, I grabbed my pillow and stumbled groggily downstairs to the car. The old man was sitting behind the wheel with the driver's side door open, smoking a Lucky and sipping his coffee.

"Almost left without you, sport," he said. "You ready to go?"

I was too tired to think of anything to say, so I just nodded.

"Well, all right then. Let's hit the road."

I threw my pillow in the back and laid everything out just so and climbed in, sleepy enough now to stretch out and go back to sleep, but too hopped up with anticipation to do anything but lie there wide awake. With the car radio playing softly, I watched the first street lamps go by one by one upside down in the window over my head, and tried to guess which streets in the neighborhood we were on. Soon enough, we were on the interstate, and as the car rocked and rolled to the rhythm of the road and the night sky grew darker, I stared up at the star-filled night, my imagination running wild among the galaxies, traveling from one wonder world to another. The next thing I knew, I was waking up to the glow of the neon lights of the all-night diner in Salisbury, Maryland. The first sliver of dawn light was barely visible above the telephone wires in the east, but there were headlights coming and going in every direction already. Stretch's Bronco and boat were wedged in the back corner of the parking lot, and the air was thick with the aromas of the ocean, coffee, and bacon grease. I was in absolute heaven!

We ate a heavy breakfast and then hit the road again, this time following Stretch and Skip in the old man's forest green Mustang, me in the front seat watching the sun rise and imagining that the world was watching us in envy as we caravanned to the shore. I hadn't slept much all night, and I eventually dozed off again, not waking up until we turned down a sandy dune-lined road and pulling up alongside a rough and weathered bait shack that doubled as the home of a longtime acquaintance of Stretch and my dad's, a man I came to know simply as old blind Bill. My father explained that after each trip he and Stretch would always weigh their catches on the dock, take pictures, and then hand over their fish to Bill. I think Bill had a wife and family, but I'm not sure.

Soon, without much help from Skip or me, Stretch and the old man had Chopper's gas cans filled up and the boat loaded with all of our gear. We were ready to head out past the salt marshes toward the shallows and depths of the channels and then beyond to the open sea and Smith Island.

The cruise out on the bay and through the backwater channels was as exhilarating an experience as I had ever hoped to have in my life. The aroma of Sea and Ski suntan lotion on my fair skin, the glare of the sun off the surface of the water, the wind through my hair and the spray of sea water in my face, the rhythmic bounce of the Starcraft across the rounded tops of the waves. It filled my senses in a way no other experience ever could.

Once we reached the island there came the chore of setting up camp. At ebb tide, the channel behind us faded into a nothingness that would firmly anchor even Chopper, loaded as she was with motor, tackle, and duffel. Skip and I were pressed into service like pack mules, dragging heavy loads up from the narrow inlet, through the salt grass and up over the crest of the dunes where our two-tent camp would face the open Atlantic Ocean for the next four days. Everything was made of canvas in those days and weighed a ton- tents, back packs, air mattresses, duffle bags -so a little hauling went a long way for a pair of scrawny though energetic nine-year-old boys. We couldn't wait to take off down the spine of the island, searching for conch shells and shipwrecks with buried treasure. Once the pup tents were staked, and the coolers and a couple of old wooden crates had been set up to shield our campfire from the incoming sea breezes, Stretch and the old man turned us loose.

"You boys need to go scrounge up as much firewood as you can," Stretch told us.

"Where are we gonna find wood?" Skip asked.

"Driftwood. There's lots of driftwood on the island. If you get lucky, you might even find an old wreck you can pull apart."

The moment he said the word "wreck" Skip and I swept up our gear nets and took off down the beach. We hadn't gotten twenty feet when my old man yelled, "Whoa! Whoa! *Whoa!* One more thing. Be back before dark. And keep an eye on the tide." He pointed down the beach toward a low sand berm in the distance that bisected the narrow island. "You see that rise down there?"

Skip and I squinted. "Uh-huh."

"Okay. That's an inlet. Right now it's low tide, so you can cross it safely because it's dry. In a couple of hours the tide'll come in and you won't have any way of getting back across. Do you understand?"

"Yes, sir."

"I want you both back here by the time the sun is about there." He pointed to a spot in the sky about an inch above the horizon. "You got it?"

We rolled our eyes. "*Yes*, sir."

We got it, all right: the irresistible urge to cross the inlet as fast as we could and start exploring the island. We raced each other down the beach, crossed the inlet (which was nothing more than a shallow ravine of moist, rippled sand) and then fanned out to search for strange and exotic shells, shipwrecks, and sunken treasure.

Three or four hours went by before either one of us even thought about what time it was. We'd been reconnoitering for so long that neither of us had any idea how long we had been gone, but it was a good bet we had pushed our luck on time. The sun had dropped a long way.

When we reached the inlet we found the ocean had seeped in while we were away; the sandy valley we had crossed earlier was a river now. Skip stood next to me at the water's edge, the channel swollen with the inflowing tide from the ocean, his mouth hanging open.

"Oh-oh."

"Yeah. Oh-oh," I echoed. I dropped my net load of conch shells and studied the situation. "Can't be that deep," I said. "Whadda ya think? Coupla feet maybe?"

Skip dropped his net full of shells too and edged his way down the sandy embankment to the water. "I don't know. Let's see." He waded into the water up to his shins, then confidently announced, "Yeah. We can cross."

Just then, I looked up and, squinting against the glare of the late afternoon sun, I saw my old man and Stretch in the distance trudging toward us. It was impossible to gauge their mood by the way they were walking, and they were too far away to read their facial expressions, but it didn't look good.

"They look mad," Skip said.

"Duh, ya think?" I said. I raised my hand to shield my eyes.

The old man yelled something, but I couldn't make out what he had said.

"What'd he say?" Skip asked.

"Beats me," I said.

"*What?*" I hollered toward my dad. He yelled again and pointed toward the ocean.

"We'd better go," Skip said.

I agreed. "Yeah, you're right," I said. "He wants us to cross before the water gets any deeper." I gathered my netful of beach combing souvenirs, and slap splashed into the water. My feet sank an inch in the sand, and I could feel the tide's gentle pull, the current at the surface pushing me inland, the flow at the bottom tugging my feet in the opposite direction toward the open ocean. Skip joined me, and we began to wade across the inlet in the open arms of the tide.

"STOP!" This time I heard the old man clearly. The wind from the ocean made his voice small. "GO BACK!" He was waving his arms frantically, and so was Stretch.

"Why?" I hollered back, and kept wading.

"Do it!" Stretch barked. "Turn around and go back!" Both men looked positively apoplectic.

"I don't get it," Skip said. "I thought he wanted us to come back."

"Me too," I said. I waded another step. The water was up to my waist now.

"STOP!" both men screamed, and waved us off.

"GET BACK UP ON THE SAND!" Stretch shrieked.

"What for?" Skip called back.

"LOOK!" My old man pointed toward the ocean, then at the current we were in.

"Yeah, I *know*. We're crossing as fast as we can."

"NO!" cried my father. "GO BACK!"

What does he want? Go back? Go back for what? I waded a little further, to the middle of the channel. The water was up to my chest, the current trying to pull my feet out from under me, when I felt something bump my leg. Instinctively, I yanked my leg away from whatever it was. Then I saw Skip an arm's length away beside me, and relaxed. It was nothing. A school of minnows, maybe, or a fish.

The old man's eyes were fierce. "Get back up on the shore this *minute*! Do you hear me? Both of you!"

"This is stupid," I muttered to Skip, reluctantly turning around and indignant in my retreat. "Whaddya want us to do," I called back, "spend the night over here?"

"I want you to stay put, that's what I want you to do," he yelled. "You'll have to wait until the tide goes out again."

I felt Skip brush past me a second time and swatted at him. "Hey, quit bumpin' into me," I said.

"I'm nowhere near you," he insisted. I turned to look at him. He was a good four or five feet away from me. Hmm. Probably a fish then. We waded back up the far shore and sat pouting on the hard-packed sand.

Stretch and the old man discussed something on the opposite bank, and after a moment my dad called out to us. "We're going back to camp to pack in our rods and check on the boat. One of us will be back in about an hour. Just stay there. Do you understand?"

"Yeah, okay" I called back. Skip waved.

"I mean it," my father said. "Stay right *there*."

"I said, *okay*. Ga!"

The two of them turned and headed south down the beach, leaving Skip and me to sit and draw pictures in the sand.

After only a couple of minutes, though, I grew bored. "Why don't we just go ahead and cross now," I said, "before the water gets too deep?"

Skip wasn't so sure. "Naw, let's just do what he says and stay here."

"They're gonna take *forever* to get back," I said. "Come on, let's cross now."

I grabbed my net of shells and walked to the water's edge. "You comin'?"

"I don't think we should."

"Then *you* stay, you little weenie. I'm goin' across."

I waded back into the water. Ankle deep . . . knee deep . . . The current pushed and pulled, but I kept my footing. Waist deep . . .

I was getting nervous, but only because I wasn't that strong a swimmer, and I worried the undertow might suck me out to sea. I checked over my shoulder and saw Skip splashing into the water behind me, obviously unhappy with his decision to follow me. Just at that moment, a shadowy form in the water passed in front of me, as swift as the current, and then disappeared into the murky depths beyond. Skip squealed. "Something bumped me!"

Startled, I turned and saw him with his arms curled above his head like a girl, stretching himself as tall in the water as he could. "It's just a fish," I said.

"It was big and heavy."

"Ha! Probably a channel bass," I snickered. "My old man's all the way down the island fishing, and the bass are *here!* Joke's on him."

The water was up to my chin, but I was in the middle of the inlet now; I was as close to the far shore as I was to the near. I stepped lightly and paddled with my free hand in the dark sea water, Skip following closely behind. Chest deep . . . waist deep . . . knee deep . . . splashes at our ankles and we were leaving clear sharp footprints in the wet sand.

Ha! I'd shown up my old man again! I knew what I was doing. I turned to Skip with a self-congratulatory grin and put my hands on my hips. "See? I told you it was nothing." We sat in the sand and waited for our fathers to return. Oh, sure, the old man would yell at us at first for crossing the channel when he'd told us not to, but he would have a whole new respect for me when he realized what I had done.

An hour later he and Stretch came marching up the beach. "I told you two to stay where you were," Stretch thundered.

"We wanted to cross before the water got too deep," I said.

The old man's eyes turned to blue flames. He circled around behind me and pulled me to my feet by the waistband of my shorts. A second later I felt a swift, hard kick to my butt.

"What was that for?" I squealed. "What'd I do?"

Stretch took hold of Skip too and hustled him back toward camp.

The old man grabbed a fistful of my neck and whipped me around. "You want to see what you did? Here! Let me show you." He aimed his finger at the center of the channel Skip and I had just crossed. "*That's* what you did!" he said.

"What about it?" I protested. "It wasn't even over my-"

Suddenly, there in the center of the inlet where Skip and I had been wading only a few minutes before, three grey triangular shapes cut through the water's surface.

"Bull sharks!" the old man growled. "I've seen five just since I walked up."

"Sharks?"

"Yes, sharks!"

The shadow? The heavy bump?

Realizing what I had just waded through, made me feel suddenly queasy.

"When I tell you to do something, mister, don't question me. Just do it! Do you understand?"

I heard what he said, but my mouth wouldn't open. I was too shocked by images of sharks and their glistening serrated teeth, along with great pools of my own blood drifting away with the tide.

"Do you have any idea how dangerous what you just did was?" the old man asked.

I stared at the flowing inlet, saw a large dorsal fin break the surface, then another, then a third. "I- we didn't know there were sharks," I said meekly.

"I know you didn't. But, I *did*. Never mind the fact you disobeyed me and Stretch, or that the inlet is full of sharks, or that the undertow alone could have pulled you out to sea." He kicked me again, harder this time. "Boy, when I tell you to do something, you do it. Don't question me!"

But you're was always saying it's good to ask questions, i thought. "Why not?" I asked.

From the expression on his face, I thought the old man was going to lose his mind right there in front of me. He caught himself though, and eased his grip on my neck. "Look," he said, "if you were in a war and your commander shouted 'DOWN!' you wouldn't say, 'Why?' would you?"

"I might."

"Judas H. Priest, boy! No, you *wouldn't*. If you did, you might be dead."

"Why?"

"Because in the time it took you to ask *why*, an enemy soldier who had you in his sights would have already pulled the trigger, that's why. It'd be too late. Do you understand?"

"But I'm not in a war. I'm on the beach."

"Jesus, Mary and Joseph! That's not the point. Believe it or not, sometimes your old man knows things you don't. Like when he tells you to stay on the beach and wait for him to come back because he knows about riptides. Because he knows sharks run in this inlet at high tide."

I didn't really understand what riptides were or what sharks in a barrier island inlet had to do with soldiers and snipers, but I nodded my head anyway. "Yeah, I guess."

"Good. Now, let's go back to camp and get some dinner." He threw his arm across my shoulder and gently guided me into an about-face. We drifted down the beach toward the incoming tide and let the advancing surf wash over our bare feet as the sun began its descent behind the sand dunes.

"Dad," I said after we had been walking for a couple of minutes, "how did you know there were sharks in the water?"

"That's a good question," he said. He thought about his answer for a minute, then stopped and turned to face the ocean. "Sometimes you just know," he said, "and sometimes you *know*. Dads who've been on the beach before *know*. And your old man's been on the beach before."

LESSON 4

Shattered

When I was in the third grade our family doctor suggested I might need to get glasses for what he suspected was a mild case of astigmatism. I didn't know what astigmatism was, but I knew glasses were a sure way to get picked on and teased at school, even if I only had to use them for reading. Right from the beginning I fought the idea and tried to talk my way out of it.

"*Other* kids wear glasses," I told my mother. Nerdy kids get stuffed in their lockers. Kids with glasses get singled out by the class clowns and bullies. Kids with glasses don't have any friends except for other nerds who wear glasses. Teachers' pets wear glasses."

"*I* was a teacher's pet," Mom said.

"That's different."

"How is it different?"

"Because you're old. You were a kid when no one was cool and it didn't matter."

"Oh. Well, that explains it."

"Please, Ma, I'm begging you, at least let me put it off until I'm in high school."

Mom gave me a warm, reassuring hug. "No one is going to ridicule you for wearing reading glasses," she said.

"You don't know Jasper Pennington. Or Glenda Haugluck. Or Babs Lowenstein. Babs Lowenstein made Jessie Holding cry just for having a Barbie lunchbox. And Jessie *never* cries."

Mom said, "You're getting glasses, and that's final."

I was mortified.

I spent the next week in desperate mental turmoil, trying to think of ways to wear my glasses and still avoid being seen wearing them, or, if I couldn't pull that off, to have a notebook full of comebacks ready for Babs Lowenstein and anyone else who might make a wisecrack about me wearing glasses. The only thing I could think of I had going for me that could possibly- *possibly* - blunt the impact of the coming social disaster was that I had begun to emerge as something of a class clown myself. Being a shy kid who was terribly afraid of rejection, I had learned early on that the best way to mask my insecurities was to make fun of the other kids first. That way, you were one up on any potential heckler. Then, if someone did say something like, "Hey, look at four-eyes Johnson!" I could not only chop him off at the zipper, I would also come across as though whatever he said didn't bother me.

In any case, I worried so much that it became ridiculous. By the time I went to the eye doctor and actually got the prescription for my glasses, though, the prospect of being called "four-eyes" didn't seem so bad. The more I thought about wearing glasses, the more the idea began to grow on me. For one thing, they would make me look smarter. I wanted attention anyway- that was why I was a class cut-up -and I figured maybe my teachers would like me better if I at least *looked* smarter. Before long, I was actually looking forward to wearing glasses.

The day I got them I ran straight from the car into the bathroom and tried them on, just to enjoy the feel of them. I remember looking at myself in the mirror and wondering who that strange, oddly intelligent-looking boy smiling back at me was. I studied my reflection and got goose bumps as I ran my fingers along the sleek, grey plastic nestled across the bridge of my nose, grazing my temples and hugging the sculpted cartilage behind my ears. I pressed a fingertip to the center of the frames to adjust them, and felt a wonderful, scary kind of thrill go through me, as if I had been touched by a faint jolt of electricity. For the first time in my life I felt truly special. I was proud of myself. I closed my eyes and for a moment pictured Mrs. Baxter and the other kids in my class the next day, gazing at me in rapt wonder when we pulled our desks in a circle and it came my time to read out loud. I would reach deftly into the cubby under my desktop, take out my thin leather glasses case, unsnap the flap, and with the aplomb of James Bond slip my new reading glasses on to the amazement and envy of all the other kids. *"Oh, wow,"* they would whisper to each other, *"look at Heath. He's got glasses. I never knew he was so smart!*

I opened my eyes and looked through the convex, fuzzy lenses. Seeing through my new glasses was going to take a little adjustment time until my eyes could focus clearly without my having to blink and squint when I first put them on. Ah, but that would happen soon enough.

I couldn't wait to get to school the next morning and put on my new glasses to do the arithmetic problems on the chalkboard even *before* reading time. I expected there would be a few giggles at first, but Mrs. Baxter was kind and fair. She would put an end to any snickering immediately. She would tell the class how intelligent I looked and remind them what a fine young man I was growing up to be.

The next morning I ran all the way to school and scarcely took the time to hang up my jacket. I went straight to my desk, sat down, and began working through the opening exercises, but without so much as a hint there was a pair of glasses in my book bag. Overnight I had developed a case of nerves and chickened out. But I'd put them on at reading time, by God.

The arithmetic problems were on the board, but Mrs. Baxter hadn't told us to start copying them yet, so I had a few minutes to gather my thoughts, review my canned comebacks, and prepare myself for the crucial moment.

When the 8:30 bell rang, Mrs. Baxter led us in the Pledge of Allegiance, took the lunch tally for "hot plates," and then instructed us to begin working on our arithmetic problems. Surreptitiously, I slipped on my glasses while everyone else was opening their binders, taking out lined notebook paper, and sharpening their pencils and started copying the problems from the blackboard onto my fresh, clean, lined sheet of notebook paper. The bending images on the paper took a little getting used to, but there was no question everything was clearer. Trying not to sneak peeks at the other kids to see if anyone was looking at me yet, I took out my ruler and drew perfect lines, sketched each number with perfect form, and did my calculations with precision. With each arithmetic problem I felt smarter, and as I came up with correct answer after correct answer, I anticipated the moment when Babs or Glenda or Jasper would notice my glasses and say something.

It was Deanie Savage, though, the loudest girl in the school, and unfortunately the cutest except for Laney Lee, who noticed first. She lay down her pencil and stared straight at me, covering her mouth as she giggled uncontrollably. Almost instantly, Babs, Jasper, Glenda, and the rest of the class looked to Deanie to see what she was laughing at. Of course she pointed at me, and like a thirty-headed amoeba the entire class turned its attention my way. The giggles rippled across the room like a stone in pond water, and naturally this caught Mrs. Baxter's attention.

"What's so amusing, class?" she asked.

"Heath's wearing glasses!" Deanie announced. She was trying not to laugh, but the pressure was too much, and she exploded in hysterics.

"He is?" asked Mrs. Baxter, her own curiosity aroused. She turned to face me. "Why, so he is!"

Chris Riglioni, who wore thick nerdy glasses himself and was already showing signs of a receding hairline, slapped his hand on his desk and broke into a high-pitched howl.

"Hey, Heath!" he called across the room, "how many fingers am I holding up?" He had only one, centrally located finger in the air at the time.

I was confused. "Huh?"

"Silly boy," said Mrs. Baxter, frowning playfully at Chris, "let's not demonstrate our lack of breeding by making obscene gestures, please, Christopher."

Riglioni stifled another burst of laughter and raised his ample eyebrows. "Yes, ma'am."

Glenda blurted out, "Hey, four eyes!" Christopher and I both turned our heads.

"Hush, Glenda!" said Mrs. Baxter. Then she turned her attention on me and with her line of vision the rest of the class's focus as well. "She was just joshing, Heath," she said. "Haven't you ever heard the expression, 'four eyes'? People with glasses see two of everything because they have *four eyes*. Get it? Get it?" She strolled to the front of the room to address the rest of the class, every one of whom was now staring in delight at me.

"Look, boys and girls! How clever! We're doing arithmetic, and here we have a problem in real life. Two eyes plus two lenses equals *four eyes*! Basic arithmetic."

The class howled.

I melted at my desk, like a pad of butter on a hot baked potato as Mrs. Baxter and the rest of the class enjoyed their little joke. I cupped my hands over my face and hid.

Mrs. Baxter raised her hand to restore order in the room. "Okay, okay, everyone. We've had our fun. Now let's all get back to work, shall we?"

I waited for the humiliation to pass. Friends were hard enough to come by at school, but now, after word of this got out to the rest of the fourth grade, I wouldn't stand a chance of making any new friends. I would be lucky to keep the handful I had. And it was all because of my stupid glasses.

I knew how much my mother loved me and that she had spent a lot of money on my new glasses. I didn't want to hurt her feelings, but I was the laughing stock of the whole class now. By lunch my name would be a joke around the entire school. So once Mrs. Baxter had restored order to the class and no one was looking, I slipped my glasses off and carefully put them back in their shiny leather case. Rather than endure another second of embarrassment, I shoved the case into the deepest recesses of my desk cubbyhole and squinted through the rest of the morning's arithmetic and spelling exercises, not to mention reading circle, and kept entirely to myself. I knew what I had to do, even though I knew it would break my mother's heart.

At recess, when the teachers were standing in a circle talking, and all the kids who weren't playing kickball or dodgeball were on the jungle gym or the swings, or playing hopscotch, I scrambled to the top of the grassy hill that paralleled the woods behind the school, and when I was sure no one was looking, I took my glasses case out of my pocket and ran my finger along its sleek top flap one last time. Then, with the aplomb of a spy about to set off hidden explosives, I unsnapped the case and took out my loathsome, hideous glasses- the source of all my shame. I held them in front of me at arm's length and admired them with a deep, sad longing that made me ache inside. Then, after a moment's final, quiet reflection, I opened my fingers and let my glasses fall to the ground at my feet. I fought back my tears, thought about how much I loved my glasses and loved my mom who had paid so much money for them, and then raised my heel with malicious intent. With as much force as i could muster, I stomped down and ground my glasses into the hard packed dirt until they shattered.

For a minute I couldn't move. All I could do was stare down at the only thing I had ever truly liked about myself: my glasses. Their sad, web-cracked lenses glinted in the sunlight, and I wondered how I could have done such a wretched thing to my innocent, faithful, *trusting* new best friends.

Even more, I wondered whether anyone would *ever* like me for me.

LESSON 5

The Atomic Meltdown of Love

Elementary school in the 1960s was different than it is today. Everyone always says it was a much simpler time, and the fact is, it *was*. Until the third grade I walked to school, usually alone, along a chain link fence with dense woods and a creek on the other side. It was a very happy time in my life. To this day I can't stroll through a flea market or an antique store and run my fingers across an old unravelling baseball glove, or heft a short, thick-handled and splintering Louisville Slugger without hearing the cheers and hoots of the neighborhood boys as we stood out in the summer fields playing pickup games of baseball. We didn't have cell phones and computers and Play Stations. We had the original Ant Farm, the Flintstones, Lincoln Logs, wax soldiers, record players, single speed bicycles, and, oh yes, *imagination*.

Fourth grade is a huge year in any kid's life because it represents his last year as a little kid. Today it's big for different reasons. These days they bump you up to that indefinable limbo known as intermediate school where the only things you learn are how to use the dirty words you heard in third grade but still don't know the meanings of and whether you're going to be a football jock or a band geek. Sad as it sounds, between the end of fourth grade and the beginning of your sophomore year in high school, you fly in an aimless intellectual holding pattern. You're expected to start thinking and acting like a young adult almost before you've even reached the starting line of puberty. But in the 60s there was no such thing as intermediate school; fifth and sixth grade were still considered elementary school. We were allowed to be kids for a lo longer.

For me, the greatest lesson I ever should have learned, and didn't, came in the fourth grade. The lesson weighed seventy-eight pounds and had huge blue eyes, as big as quarters. Her name was Laney Lee.

My mother always said I had a big heart, but that I put it out there for anybody to break, and that someday I was going to regret it. She may have been right. From the very first second I laid eyes on Laney Lee in the first grade I knew I was in love. Now, I know what you're thinking. You're thinking, what does a nine-year-old kid know about love? A nine-year-old knows love when he feels it, that's what, and I felt it. I had all the symptoms: lying awake at night thinking about her, staring at the moon, hungry but not eating, songs on the radio starting to make sense, fantasizing about holding her hand . . . Oh, I was in love, all right. The problem was, my little angel didn't even know I existed. It didn't help, either, that I was excruciatingly shy. If a pretty girl so much as looked my way, I turned to butter.

For one thing, I didn't have a very high opinion of myself. I was short for my age, a little bowlegged, and I had the same spray of freckles across my nose as Jared Schwartz, the little booger-eating redhead in corduroys no one wanted to sit with on the bus. I didn't have the same carrot-colored hair Jared had, with that ridiculous curling lock in the front that looked like a breaking wave in Maui, but we *did* share the same pasty white complexion. In fact, I was so self-conscious about my inability to tan in the summer that I'd wear blue jeans instead of shorts when it was ninety degrees out just to hide my pale skinny legs. Everyone knows that girls- even blonde spindly legged bucktoothed versions of future women like Laney Lee -avoid boys who aren't tall and bronze. It didn't help, either, that I had a crooked front tooth that made me extremely self-conscious and terribly afraid to smile.

On the other hand, girls, to me, were like rare, untouchable diamonds: beautiful, elusive, the source of envy and longing in the deepest recesses of my heart. Alas, they were meant for someone else, not me. The taunting teardrop curves of their eyes, the fluid, perfect seams of their warm lips, the sweet cotton candy aroma of their hair; skin so soft and unblemished they might well have been airbrushed images. In short, girls drove me absolutely crazy.

By the start of fourth grade, I had been worshipping Laney Lee from afar for three years- ever since the first grade -but I had always lacked the courage to speak to her. The very thought of speaking to Laney made my tongue dry and my palms sweat. Now, here we were in class together again in the fourth grade, but after this year there was a good chance we would wind up in different schools, in different fifth grades, separated forever because we lived in different neighborhoods. It was this year or never. Declare my love for my beautiful, thin, knobby-kneed, blonde-on-blonde beauty Laney Lee, or live the rest of my life wondering if my unrequited love might have been returned if only I had let her know how I felt about her.

There were so many changes that year: harder arithmetic problems; a screwy and confusing color-coded reading program called the SRA; loudmouthed Deanie Savage, my female competition for class clown, got braces (she was the first in our class); and recess was only once a day instead of twice.

And then there was gym class.

Until the fourth grade we had always followed the natural order in gym class: boys with boys, girls with girls: dodgeball, kickball, soccer, the President's fitness test, all the usual running around silliness that passed for physical education. Suddenly, we were confronted with a wholly inexplicable and unnecessary shakeup of the regular routine. Our gym teacher, Miss Flank, introduced us to square dancing.

Swing your partner round and round. Promenade. Do-si-do.

Not just dancing- *square* dancing. Something no G. I. Joe-outfitting, Wolf badge-earning Cub Scout would be caught dead doing if the gym teacher didn't make him do it.

Except me. I confess I secretly liked it. Why? Well, the answer's obvious: because our iron maiden gym instructor Miss Flank forced us into circles of eight in boy-girl-boy-girl order. That meant girls who would otherwise never have come within ten yards of me had to stand beside me and hold my hand.

"Everybody grab a partner!" Miss Flank would order us.

Oh, boy! A partner!

I'd look in every direction for Laney and try to hide my enthusiasm, only to discover she was on the other side of the gym, standing next to Luther Schmaltz or that smelly behemoth Bruce Durtz. Meanwhile, some other girl who nobody else wanted to dance with would walk over to me, and with an expression that radiated the message *I'm desperate; you're all that's left*, would turn to me and say with no semblance of interest, "You wanna be partners? Or what?" Disappointed yet again that Laney had not so much as looked my way, I would smile my crooked smile and say, "Yeah, okay."

What I really wanted to do was cry out, "Laney, I love you! Come dance with me!" Instead, I stood passively, dying inside minute by minute as I watched that ogre Bruce Durtz rub shoulders with the angel the universe had set aside for *me*.

Then Miss Flank would blow her whistle and call out, "Now, everybody hold hands!" This positively sent me into orbit. If the girl next to me was even halfway cute, I immediately began to believe that she and I would wind up boyfriend and girlfriend by the end of the class period. No girl had *ever* held my hand before. Now a girl- a living, breathing *girl* -was going to hold my hand, even if she didn't want to.

But it was Laney Lee I ached for, Laney Lee I tried to maneuver close to every day in gym class, and it was Laney I never got to hold hands with. If Laney ever did stand next to me on the gym floor when partners were randomly assigned for the Virginia Reel, well then, she would *have* to hold my hand.

Sometimes, while we waiting for Miss Flank to start the record on the phonograph, I would pretend that Laney and I were holding hands, walking along the sands of a moonlit beach. Our hearts swelling in anticipation of a soft romantic kiss. Laney would coyly bring our stroll to a halt, look up into my misting eyes, and whisper, "I love you, Heath . . ."

The fantasy nearly made me cry, right there in the middle of gym class. For a moment, just an instant, I would suddenly have the courage to speak to Laney, to tell her how I really felt. No more slumping in my desk playing the ignore game, the one where I would look at her from across the room until she caught me doing it and then, in a flash, look away, pretending I was looking at something else. No sir, no more. I had loved Laney for too long, and she had never known it.

This went on for the entire fall and and winter until, one day in the spring, our class was sitting at the lunch table in the cafeteria, the way we did every day at eleven-thirty, eating together with our teacher Mrs. Davis. Even though we were required to sit together and eat lunch as a class, and even though the tables were the kind that folded in half and had those uncomfortable, permanently attached little round stools for seats, it had never once worked out that Laney and I sat next to or across from other. I'd have probably thrown up out of sheer panic if we had. But on this particular day the planets were aligned and the only seat left at the table by the time I got my ice cream and came looking for a place to sit, was right across from Laney. I was so excited my heart flopped like a fish; I couldn't breathe. Trembling, I slid my metal Flintstones lunch box on the table and sat down across from her, trying desperately not to make eye contact with her. After all, if she had seen *me* seeing *her*, she would have gotten the idea that I liked her and had sat across from her on purpose. I certainly couldn't risk *that*.

I didn't say a word; this was the ignore game at a professional level. I had no idea what to say anyway. She was cheerily talking to her friends and didn't seem to notice me- the usual encounter -when the oddest thing happened. Right after I sat down, Laney's little clique got up to go outside. The kids on either side of me got up as well and dashed outside for recess. It was as if everyone around us had heard a secret message telling them to get up and leave Laney and me alone. It was the weirdest thing. One minute we were surrounded by classmates, and the next minute we were sitting across from each other in the most awkward silence imaginable.

Laney and me alone.

My knees were knocking, but thank goodness she couldn't see them under the table, though she *could* see my shaking hands as I finished my ice cream sandwich. Laney just sat there, watching me, meticulously folding her napkin. Paralyzed with fear, I pretended not to notice. My mind was racing, scrambling for the right combination of moves and words. *Should I say something? Should I look at her? Or should I play it cool and get up to go outside? What's the use? She doesn't even know I'm alive. But what if she asks me to stay?*

I finished my ice cream sandwich and gulped down the last of the milk in my Thermos.

"Hi, Heath," said Laney.

Stunned, I glanced up at her, but only for a second. She was looking right at me! I lowered my eyes to my lap and studied my shaking hands. "Oh. Hi."

Laney giggled. I felt as though I was melting off my seat, but Laney was locked onto me, her crystalline blue eyes holding me in place. I wondered if I should try to say something clever to make her laugh. Yes, but what if I said the wrong thing and she *didn't* laugh? Then she would think I was a nerdinski for sure. I twirled my lunch box in a slow circle on the table, waiting for her to say something else.

Then she smiled.

I smiled back.

"Heath," she said, "have you ever had a girlfriend?"

Had I ever had a girlfriend? What kind of question was that? Where did *that* come from?

Immobilized with panic, I tried to think how I should answer, but my mind had gone blank. My head was a great dark cave echoing the *drip, drip, drip* of eternity. For a millisecond my gaze locked onto Laney's huge pleading blue eyes. I felt feverish, and my tongue felt as though it was coated with sawdust. With the stunned uncertainty of a deer caught in the headlights, I went with the first- the *only* -thought that surfaced from the abysmal recesses of my mind: I shook my head no.

"Would you *like* a girlfriend?" she said, obviously undaunted and determined to extract me from the deep lair of my shyness. She smiled coyly and batted her eyelashes.

I felt as though I had swallowed a large rubber kickball. How do you answer a question like *that*? Was she doing what girls always did, setting me up with false hope so she could yank the rug out from under me at the last second and humiliate me in front of God, the school, and the entire world? Laney would never do that. Would she?

I stalled.

"Huh? A-" I tried to appear nonchalant, just in case, but the truth is I was too excited to care. Too excited to think straight. Too excited to overcome my fear of rejection. Flustered, I eyed the playground outside.

"Would you *like* a girlfriend?" she repeated, this time with just the slightest hint of urgency.

My mind raced. *Love. Rejection? Does she mean it? Is she setting me up? Love forever? Heartbreak forever? What do I say? What do I do?*

In a moment I cannot say even today was guided by common sense or clarity, I calmly put my empty Thermos bottle back in my lunch box, latched the clasp on the front of the box, and with as much aplomb as a terrified, lovestruck fourth grade boy can summon, looked her right in her big, beautiful eyes and said,

"No."

Laney's smile vaporized. My own heart sank. I felt stupid and cowardly. The instant the word "no" came out of my mouth I wanted to take her in my arms and plead with her: *I didn't mean it, Laney! I didn't mean it! I was just kidding!*

This was the atomic meltdown of love. The Great Disaster. There was no unringing this bell. Laney looked stunned, as full of hurt and dejection as *I* had ever been. She didn't say another word. Instead, she lowered her eyes sadly as I, even more stunned than she was at what I had just heard myself say and kicking myself for saying it, took my lunch box in both hands and ran outside without looking at her again.

Outside on the playground, all the other kids were playing kickball, swinging on the jungle gym, running around and chasing each other, everyone having a great time at recess, oblivious to the intense pains of love. I, on the other hand, was sick to my stomach. I wandered over to the low berm at the edge of the playground where the school property met the surrounding woods, at almost the same spot where I had crushed my glasses in the dirt the year before, and stood in dumb amazement at my own blunder.

Why did you say no? "Would you like a girlfriend?" she asked. And you told her no! The one girl in the world you love more than anything asks you to be her boyfriend, and you say no! Everybody's right. You are *a dork.*

I was upset the whole afternoon and didn't speak to anyone, not even Mrs. Davis. The one time I snuck a glance in Laney's direction that afternoon she was working quietly at her desk, her downcast eyes staring at her assignment book, her pencil idly doodling on her paper.

And that's how it was for the rest of the school year: Laney not seeming to know or care if I was even alive, me suffering silently, daily, always wondering what might have been. A thousand times I tried to summon the courage to go up to her and say, *"Laney, I love you. I do want a girlfriend. I want you! I want you so bad!"*

But I was too afraid and kept my distance. Laney Lee never knew how much I adored her, that little freckle faced Heath Johnson had an enormous, debilitating crush on her.

C'est la vie, no?

Then it came: the last day of school. I wouldn't see Laney at all during the summer, and by the time we were in fifth grade in the fall she would have given up on me entirely. Worse, she would have forgotten me altogether. We would probably be in different schools, and Laney would never ever know of my hopeless, tireless, breathless love for her. Though I would never, *never* stop loving her, I had doomed myself to live in silent agony forever.

That afternoon, as everyone else was celebrating the end of school and the start of summer, I stood alone at the bike rack, dejected, lonely, heartbroken, aching to see Laney one more time. I was dying to run up to her run up to her and shout out, *Yes, yes, yes! I'll be your boyfriend, Laney! I promise I'll never say no to you again. Not for the rest of my life!*

Did I have the courage? If I saw her, would I be brave enough to risk humiliation and rejection? Would I have the nerve to tell her what was in my heart, what had *always* been in my heart since the first day I had laid eyes on her?

Yes! Yes! A thousand times, yes! *Please, God, just let me find her before she gets on her bus and leaves my life forever.*

I searched the milling crowds of kids to catch a glimpse of Laney one last time, to touch her golden heart with my thoughts so she would know, but I never saw her. She never got on her bus. When the buses started their engines and began to pull away like a line of lumbering bumble bees, I knew I had missed my last chance with Laney. She was gone for the summer. Between now and the start of school in the fall she would have new adventures, go to new and exciting places, go swimming and playing with her friends. All without me; without even a *thought* of me. Worst of all, she would probably have a boyfriend in the fall. After all, I wasn't the only boy in the fourth grade who had noticed those big beautiful blue eyes, her long golden hair, her cute clothes and her heavenly fragrance. Other wolves had caught the scent and had started to flirt with her by the end of school. I had *no* chance now. None. And it was my own stupid fault.

I had just turned to unlock my bicycle from the bike rack, trying to disguise my sniffling teary eyes from anyone who might be watching, when I was startled by a mild tap on the shoulder. I wheeled around to see who it was and came face-to-face with Laney. She stood small before me and handed me a note folded into one of those compact triangles girls spend an entire class period folding and that take forever to unfold. "This is for you," she said.

I was speechless, in total shock. Laney had written a note to *me*? To *me*, Heath Johnson? The kid who told her he didn't want a girlfriend? My heart leapt. I broke into a ridiculous, irresistible grin. "What's this?" I asked her.

"Just read it," she said. Then she turned and walked away toward the car line where her mother was waiting. Right then I knew- I *knew* -that Laney liked me enough to have gotten past my idiotic response at lunch three months before and had written me a note to say so. A note from Laney could only mean one thing: it was going to be a long, fabulous, lonely summer, but at least now I could spend those long hot dreary months dreaming about the love of my life knowing that come the fall she would be girlfriend for real. My dream would be true. Emboldened by the note in my hand, I called after her, "Hey, Laney-" But she never looked back, she just kept walking. When she reached her car, she got in and they drove away.

Goodbye, Laney Lee. I hope- I hope you won't forget me.

I was stupid with joy. I stuffed the note in my pocket and raced home on my bike. I couldn't wait to read what she had written. When I got home I raced upstairs and tucked the note under my pillow, determined to savor every minute, every second, of my unimaginable good fortune. The anticipation was killing me, but through sheer willpower I was going to force myself to wait until bedtime to read the sacred words of Laney Lee, the love of my life.

The hours crawled by, century slow. Eventually, nine o'clock came, and I kissed my mother and the old man goodnight.

"What's the hurry, sport?" my father asked with a tousle of my hair. "It's summer. You can stay up an hour later if you want to."

"Yeah, I know, Dad. But I'm, uh, I'm awfully tired. I'm just gonna turn in and get a fresh start on my vacation."

As soon as Mom flicked out the light and closed my bedroom door I took out my Cub Scout flashlight to read Laney's note. My hands trembled; after all, I had said no to her.

I sniffed the paper and caught a whiff of her aroma. With supreme care and precision I opened the note. It was written in pen. Purple pen! That meant that whatever she had written was meant to be permanent. It was forever. And it was written in real *girl* handwriting with flowers over the "i's" and puppy faces after each period.

I read the note slowly, then did what I had done so many times because of my love for Laney Lee: I cried. I went back over each word, each syllable, one at a time, but the note was short. Painfully short. My hands shook, my heart fluttered. After half a dozen readings I put the note down and wondered again what it would be like to hold Laney's soft hand on a starry moonlit night. To have her look adoringly into my eyes and say, "I love you, Heath Johnson."

I sat by my window and hung my chin on the edge gazing up at the moon for half the night. Eventually, I grew too tired to keep my eyes open any longer, so I folded the note back up perfectly, precisely, just the way Laney had folded it, and placed it under my pillow. Clutching it for safekeeping, I lay my head on the pillow and fell asleep with images of Laney dancing in my mind.

In the morning the first thing I did when I woke up was feel the folded paper in my hand under my pillow. I had to read it one more time, just to make sure I hadn't dreamed the whole thing.

Carefully, I unfolded the paper and read it one last time.

Heath,

I am moving to California over the summer. I wanted to be your girlfriend because I love you, Heath Johnson. I thought you loved me too, but I was wrong.

I will always miss you, always and forever.

Laney Lee,

Your never-was girlfriend.

LESSON 6

Solace

Other than one or two very hazy slide show images of a zoo that occasionally slip up through the floor boards of my memory, I don't recall having many up-close encounters with animals when I was a kid. I'm sure I watched squirrels scampering up tree trunks, and of course there were birds everywhere- I didn't grow up in a cave -but what I'm saying is that I didn't have any real contact with animals when I was little. We lived in apartments, so the prospects of having a family pet, other than my kid brother, were as far away as the dark side of the moon.

When my family moved to Somerville, New Jersey, shortly after my eighth birthday, however, we lived in a house for the first time. The neighborhood was arranged in such a way that every homeowner had an acre of yard, and every yard backed up to three others so that everyone had the illusion of owning four acres, dotted here and there with clusters of young spruce and cedars. Believe it or not, this was my introduction to living in the country. People don't think of New Jersey as being rural, but the fact is parts of the state are actually quite rustic and beautiful. I guess this semi-pastoral setting enriched my father's dreamscape as much as it did mine because in very short order after we moved into our house he bought a lawn tractor, some garden tools, and one Friday night caught my brother, my mother, and me completely by surprise when he walked through the front door with a puppy, a cuddly mutt as black as night with a white stripe down his front, leaping and hopping as if he were hard wired to the wall socket.

"What in the world?" my mother asked, walking out from the kitchen with a spaghetti ladle dangling from her fingers.

The old man deadpanned his answer. "Well, I'm not sure, but I think it's a dog."

My brother and I fell to our knees and took turns gathering the yipping, twirling, bouncing little pup in our arms. It was hard to tell who was more excited, David and me, or the puppy; all three of our tails were wagging ninety-nine to nothing.

"Do we get to keep him, Dad?" I asked, squinting and puckering defensively as the puppy licked my face repeatedly with his warm wet tongue.

The psycho pup broke free from my grasp and ran in miniature concentric circles, his tiny feet slipping and sliding out from under him on the hardwood floor, and tangling himself up in the leash, all the while nipping joyously at anyone and everything within his reach.

"He's ours," said my father.

"Forever?" David asked as he bent down to try to unwrap the leash from around the puppy's feet.

"Forever's a long time," said my dad. "But, yes, he's ours. He's a member of our family now."

"Whatever possessed you?" Mom asked.

The old man handed the leash to me. "Here, you hold him," he said. "I don't know. I just felt it was time the boys had a dog. Every boy needs a dog."

"I suppose," said Mom. "Where you'd get him?"

"Rich Phipps down at the office. Sadie had a litter last month, and Rich has been trying to find homes for the pups for a couple of weeks. This is the last of the brood."

"What're we gonna name him?" David asked.

My father reached down to the puppy and unclipped the leash. "Here, why don't we let him loose so he can explore and learn his way around? Well, I was hoping maybe you and Heath would come up with a good name for him."

"How about Shazam?" asked David.

"What, are you nuts?" I said. "You don't name a dog Shazam. What kind of stupid name is that?"

"It's not stupid! I like it."

My dad stepped in at precisely the right moment to prevent another pointless argument. "On second thought, let's let Mom name him," he said.

"Me?" my mother said, looking a little flustered.

"Why not?" said the old man.

"Yeah! You name him!" David said gleefully.

I could tell Mom was taken aback by this sudden responsibility, yet she seemed happy enough to be the one to make the first executive decision about the family dog. She thought a moment, then hit on an idea.

"You know who's going to wind up doing all the work taking care of this dog, don't you?" she said. "Me, that's who."

"No, mom," I protested, "David and I'll take care of him. We'll feed him and walk him and wash him and everything."

"Walk him, eh?" she said with a cautious half-smile. "We'll see."

"So," said the old man, "what're you going to name him?"

Without missing a beat, and as if she had had the name picked out and ready to go for ages, Mom lifted the slap happy pup to eye level and rubbed his nose with hers. "Prince," she said. "We'll call him Prince."

And so, for the next five years and sixty-five pounds, Prince took his rightful place on the throne as the fifth and arguably most important member of our family. Never asking for anything more than the opportunity to chase a tennis ball in the backyard until he collapsed from exhaustion, or a walk through the snow drifts on a cold wintery night, Prince was the delight of our lives, a true friend to us all. But none more, I think, than me. He was the one "person" in the house I could tell my secrets to, the only one who would curl up with me on the den floor and watch cartoons at six in the morning on Saturdays. For the pure joy of entertaining me, he would sit up and beg on command, even if I had no treat to give him, but more than anything he was my friend, a playmate keen to take the other end of a hand towel and play tug of war with.

In the winter of that year, when Annie Newdecker, who lived two houses down from us, and I officially became boyfriend and girlfriend in the seventh grade, Prince was my excuse (and Holly, Annie's insane black Labrador, her excuse) to go walking in the foot-deep snow at night so that she and I could have romantic trysts without her parents getting suspicious.

Because we lived in a neighborhood where there were only two streets and each one intersected with the other one, and both were dead end cul-de-sacs that butted up to the Willis farm's lower cow pasture, we would let Prince out at night to go explore and romp, knowing that an hour later he would show up at the back door, his tongue flopping out the side of his mouth, his chest heaving, and an exuberant gleam in his eyes that said, *Oh man, you would not believe where I've been tonight!* Except that on those nights when he ventured into the Willis's field and rolled in the cow patties, we knew exactly where he had been, and we'd have to hose him off at ten o'clock at night in the backyard. But, that was Prince: a powder keg of energy, certifiably amuck with love, as touchingly free as the wind. My first best friend.

Then, one night it happened.

It was after dark and after dinner. Mom asked me to let Prince out for his nightly run, and I was no sooner at the backdoor than that crazy dog came skidding around the corner and slammed into me and the door both, jumping with all four feet off the ground and snapping at the air as he yelped with excitement.

Yippee! Woo-hoo! I get to go out now! I get to go out!

I always loved being the one who got to let Prince out at night because it made me his hero; he associated me with his nightly romps, which of course made me special in his eyes, and I needed that.

I opened the door and Prince took off into the dark as if he'd been fired from a gun. "So much for being happy here, you deranged mutt," I said as he took off into the night. I flicked on the back porch light, and went inside to do my homework.

Half an hour later I heard the screech of tires out in front of the house, followed a minute later by a commotion downstairs. Something exciting was going on, and I didn't want to miss it. David and I converged at the top of the stairs simultaneously and ran down to the laundry room together to see what all the ruckus was about. We arrived just as my father was opening the door and my mother snatching towels in a panic from the cabinet over the washing machine. One glance out the back door to the cement landing in the floodlight and I knew we had a serious family crisis at hand. Prince lay across the stoop, panting rapidly, still up on his forelegs, as if he had returned home exhausted from his adventures and had decided to lie down and rest before coming inside. *That's not like him*, I thought. Then, a second, closer look showed me why he was resting there, and I nearly fainted.

Prince's chest was torn open, ripped down the middle of his white stripe from shoulders to sternum. I could see everything. My father worked feverishly to wrap towels around Prince, and Mom helped. I was grateful they were covering up the mess because I couldn't stand to see my best friend torn open that way and suffering, but also because I naively believed that if my dad just wrapped enough towels around Prince the bleeding would stop the bleeding and he would heal, as good as new in no time.

And that's what more or less happened. My father rushed our mortally wounded dog to the veterinarian's office while my mother stayed home to call Doctor Cooper and tell him that my father was on the way to the clinic and would be there in about ten minutes. When she hung up the phone she pulled David and me close and wept softly, and because she cried, we cried too.

Several hours later, long after our usual bedtime, the old man came home with the hopeful news that Doctor Cooper had performed surgery on Prince and that Prince was not only still alive, but stable. He would know more in the morning.

Well, Prince did survive, and he lived for a very long time indeed. Seventeen and a half years, in fact. He went on to chase many, many more tennis balls, but he never knew the ecstasy of moist cow dung again because we never let him loose again.

Eventually, the time came when Prince grew too old and sore to chase tennis balls and play tug-of-war, or even to enjoy living anymore; he told us so with his sad eyes and his creaking bones. More than once we talked as a family about the approaching and inevitable end of his life, when and how it would be handled, how we felt about it, what our house was going to be like without him, and why is it a dog doesn't get to live very long yet still has to die old. Dad explained to David and me how a situation like this was usually handled. Even though I was twenty-five by this time and David twenty-one, this was as unfamiliar and unsettling to us as if we were toddlers. Emotionally, we wanted no part of it, but intellectually we handled the discussions stoically. It was what our father hoped and expected of us. It was the only way we could deal with it without breaking down.

Then one evening, just like that, it was done. My father took Prince to Doctor Cooper's office after dinner, and half an hour later he was in the backyard digging a hole, the clean white pine box he had spent the previous weekend building resting beside the ever-growing mound of dirt he was shoveling out of the ground. I had seen death before- my grandmother died when I was twelve, my great grandmother when I was ten -but while those realities were enough to make an impression on me, there's nothing quite like having the daily attachment of a beloved pet forcibly wrenched away from you and buried in the ground. I told myself Prince had lived a good long happy life, and he had, but that did nothing to take way the sense of loss and sorrow.

Ten years went by and I had moved to Houston by the time I got my second dog, a gangly Labrador-Doberman mix I called Larry Bird, named after my mother's favorite basketball player. He was a rescue dog, as black as Prince, who had been thrown out the window of a passing pickup truck as a puppy and left to fend for himself. I didn't have a family at the time, and I guess I was looking for a friend, so Larry Bird came to live with me.

L.B. and I went everywhere together, did everything together. Just as I had done with Prince when I was a kid, I was even able to turn him loose in the woods and in fields, and even though he might disappear for an hour or more, he would always turn up just about the time I was beginning to worry. He was all you'd ever want in a dog: friendly, warm, strong, gentle, loyal, and just dumb enough to fail obedience school and just smart enough to steal your heart. Years later, when I got married and began to raise a family, L.B. took them all in and made them his own. He was just that way.

But I had forgotten that dogs don't live forever. One day I noticed: Larry Bird's muzzle had turned white, and he had slowed down. The field where I used to sit on a small hill and watch him sniff out rabbits had been overtaken by a city works center and a Quick Mart gas station. Where the railroad tracks once marked the end of the hunt, a new crossing and a new road that bisected our field made it too hazardous to let him run free anymore. My wild times with L.B. were done.

Instead, our quiet times came more and more frequently. There was a sadness in L.B.'s eyes I had never seen before, I could see it when he lay at my feet; he would look up at me sometimes as if to say, "Heath, I'm whipped. I'm ready to call it a day."

I pretended not to notice the slowness in his gait, the pain in his standing, the whiteness creeping across the tops of his paws and on the tip of his tail. I took him to our old field, or what was left of it, but he didn't seem interested. I couldn't blame him. I wanted to play, but he seemed to always be sleeping and couldn't collect the energy to indulge me. Sometimes it was all he could do to get up and walk to his dish to eat. Some days it was all I could do to admit that my dear friend was ready to leave me. In a kind of desperate attempt to change his mind I would lie on the floor beside him late at night and run my hand along his back, whispering, reminding him of all the adventures we had shared over the years. Reminding him how much he was loved and wanted, at that moment and from the beginning.

Larry Bird loved me, I know that, and so for my sake he hung on. When he had barely the strength to open his eyes and wag his tail he gave me solace.

Heath, I'm tired. I'm so very, very tired. Please let me go.

I didn't want to let him go, but his lusterless eyes and a diagnosis of terminal cancer by our family veterinarian put the matter to rest. How I wished my old man could be the one to spirit L.B. away in the car and it would all be done, out of my sight. I would only have to deal with the void.

But I was the father now, and there would be no spiriting away the dying dog. My wife and two young boys said their goodbyes, and L.B. and I walked to the car. Our appointment with Dr. Cooper was set 4:00, but we left early so L.B. and I could have one last walk in the park, one last quiet, minor adventure.

Oh, it was a beautiful afternoon! We had a wonderful walk, and wouldn't you know it? L.B. perked up; he sniffed everything, wagged his tail constantly, and had me second guessing my decision to have him put down. Had I jumped too soon? Was he miraculously getting better? Just as we had done a thousand times before, L.B. and I took in the sights and sounds and smells of the tiny moments of beautiful, beautiful life.

Half an hour later I did exactly what my old man had had to do with Prince over twenty years before: I held L.B.'s head in my lap and looked into his soulful brown eyes as they slowly closed and life silently slipped out of the room.

LESSON 7

Our Town

In Somerville, the unassuming north central town in New Jersey where I grew up in the 1960s, we had a little bit of everything. We had diners, gas stations, a Gaston's Department store, a few doctors' and dentists' offices, a small post office, a Bowl-R-Rama, and a drive-in movie theater. The population was mixed: whites, blue collar and white collar, Italians, Puerto Ricans, Jews, Pollocks, blacks, Asians, Irish, Catholic, Irish-Catholic . . . You name the ethnic group, I lived with them, went to school with them, shopped with them, played with them, laughed with them, rode bicycles with them, shared secrets with them, went trick-or-treating with them.

You would think that a boy growing up with that kind of ethnic diversity would almost be oblivious to the differences, the way a kid who grows up with first generation immigrant parents and hears mostly Spanish or Italian at home, say, can't hear his father's accent when he speaks English. But it wasn't that way for us. We were always very aware of the ethnic differences between us, the white kids, and everybody else who didn't look or sound like us. Maybe it was a generational thing, or maybe it was bred into our genes to take special notice of and be cautious around anyone who didn't look, act, or sound like us. I would love to tell you I was color blind; none of us were.. Neither was any other kid I knew. The jokes and shots flew fast, furiously and often, and everyone was fair game. Right or wrong, that was just how it was back then. Stereotypes existed for a reason, and as a middle class white kid I never tired of pointing out the shortcomings in everyone else, especially anyone who wasn't white.

Somerville was like any small town; it had its heroes and its jerks, its geniuses and its morons. And like many small American towns, its history suggested that one or two prominent families had been there from the inception and that the town itself had evolved outwardly from those original homesteads. If you went into Gaston's Department Store downtown, or one of the better-known restaurants around town, as likely as not in any conversation you would hear the name of one of those families. In Somerville, Willis and Silver were the two names you heard most often.

Where I lived the houses were a little farther apart and set farther back from the road than the houses closer to town. Our neighborhood backed up to one of the Willis farm's fields where old man Willis turned his Angus out in the morning and where Prince rolled in their dung at night. We had woods nearby, a creek, small country roads, a few red barns with hex signs over the doors, a white steepled Methodist church, and Martins" Market, the little mom and pop country store near the river that had been a fixture in the area before the Hoover administration and was a favorite hangout for kids in the summer. I was growing up in two very distinct yet cultural environments: Norman Rockwell's idyllic rural America and the turbulent, psychedelic 1960s.

Every day when I went to school, I *went* to school. I never gave any thought to what races of kids were going to be in class with me, or whether they greased their hair back or put it in a pony tail or braided it or stuck a fork in it. I didn't care if they wore a hijab, had an ash spot on their forehead, wore a star of David necklace, went to church over the weekend, or could only spell "dumb" if you spotted them the first three letters and gave them clues to help them with the "b". I knew it took all kinds to make up our town and our school, but I really didn't care, not on a conscious level, anyway. School's just a microcosm of the town you live in, and back then who paid attention to anybody who didn't live in your neighborhood?

Going all the way back to elementary school and with roots penetrating deep into the social loam of high school, there was one family tree that stood apart from all the others in our town, and that was the Silver family tree. With brothers and sisters and aunts and uncles and grandparents and cousins, the Silver family seemed to be everywhere. So established was the clan in fact that they lived in their own section of Somerville named after them and known informally as "Silvertown." Silvertown was where all the Silver relatives lived, of course, but it was also where most of the other black families lived as well. It was a peculiar fact of the times, I thought, that none of us in my neighborhood ever saw any of the Silver clan- or any of the other black kids or their families either for that matter -anywhere around town, on the weekends, in the summer, nor even at Christmas. It occurred to me more than once that I ought to have run into members of a family as large and well known as the Silvers all over town, but I never did.

The Silvers were said to be able to trace their origins back to the days of the Civil War, but whether they were descendants of slaves or land owners, I don't know. How they came to be in Somerville first, I don't know either. One thing I do know is that they had a reputation for being kind, friendly, churchgoing people. Everyone who knew the Silvers liked them.

That was certainly true for me, though I never knew any of the family except for Lonnie, a stocky boy my age who became my friend in the fifth grade, though exactly how we came to know each other is a mystery to me now. I'm not sure I knew the particulars even back then. It might be that we just sort of fell in with each other on the playground; many friendships happened that way. It might have been during a game of kickball, or a group of boys standing around the backstop. Who knows?

What I do remember- and this is an odd fact, I think -is that I was very proud to be seen with Lonnie Silver, as if I were showing him off.

Look at me, everybody, Heath Johnson is pals with Lonnie Silver, the most popular black kid in school.

I wasn't proud to call Lonnie my friend *only* because he was black, or because his last name was Silver, though both facts were guaranteed to work in my favor when it came to my tenuous social standing. I think, on some deep emotional, psychological level I *was* proud of myself for making friends with a black kid, as if by accepting Lonnie as my friend I had somehow proven myself to be racially open minded and therefore somehow better than those who didn't have a black friend. After all, this was the mid 60s, and race relations in America hadn't changed much since Restoration. To pal around with a black kid and actually *like* him, well, that said something good about me. I was the accepting, tolerant, open-minded white kid. The flower power mantra of peace, love, and happiness hadn't been lost on me.

One day my friendship with Lonnie paid huge dividends that I could never have foreseen. Surprisingly, we didn't have many black kids at Mountain View Junior High, but of the ones I knew, Lonnie was by far the friendliest and best liked. A few of the others weren't so friendly, and for whatever reason one of them, Stanley Murdock, a brooding, powerfully built thug who was none too bright (and was happy enough to show off his impressive lack of intelligence to any class that would give him the attention he wanted), and for some inexplicable reason he had it out for me. I didn't even know the guy, only his name and reputation, though I later theorized that he had me in his crosshairs precisely *because* I was friends with Lonnie. In Stanley's mind blacks and whites were only supposed to mingle if they were in a fist fight. Anyway, one day at recess Stanley was standing out by the monkey bars when he spotted me and started walking in my direction, his eyes locked on me like heat-seeking missiles, his fists clenched hard and tight as sledgehammers.

"C'mere," he ordered, as he closed in on me.

Blithely, I looked around in the vain hope that he was targeting someone else in my vicinity. "Who, me?" I said.

"I'm gone whup you!" he said, the expression on his face as fierce and threatening as any I had ever seen. By now he was only a couple of steps away from me.

"W-what'd I do to you?" I pleaded.

"Yo' a stupid lookin' white boy, dat's what you done," he said.

I could feel my vital organs seizing, but I tried to look cool and unperturbed in spite of my fear. "Leave me alone," I implored, a detectable strain of panic in my voice.

"Ah, yo' *scared*, ain't you?"

"Don't make me laugh," I said defiantly, my voice cracking.

"You tough, are ya?" he growled. "Lessee how tough you is. Ah'm gone whup you rat here 'n rat now."

Before I could take my next terrified breath, Murdock scooped me up and flung me over his shoulder, his bulging biceps glistening with sweat. A crowd of kids gathered, some laughing, most just watching, no doubt relieved that Murdock had chosen me and not them. To this day I have a visual in my mind of flopping helplessly, draped over Stanley Murdock's shoulder, terrified and helpless as this much bigger and stronger black kid I am already afraid of and am instantly learning to hate carries me to whatever corner of the playground he's chosen to make an example of me. All I can see are his corduroy pants bottoms and the tawny dirt of the playground rolling away as all the other kids gather behind us and then follow like mice to the Pied Piper to watch Stanley have his way with me. Then, I see Lonnie Silver coming up from behind and telling Murdock to put me down. Stanley wheels around, the earth below spins clockwise, a blur of faces surrounding us, and the entire memory comes eerily, uneasily back into focus.

"Da hell you say!" Murdock says to Lonnie.

"The hell I say," Lonnie answers, standing toe-to-toe with Murdock.

"You gone make me?" Murdock challenges Lonnie, puffing out his chest.

"Ain't gonna have to," Lonnie says, "'cause you're gonna put my fren' down right now."

I can feel the tension in Murdock's shoulders; he is nervous and coiling, ready to strike. "Ain't gone do no such thing," he says.

"Yeah, you are."

A tense moment of silence follows and then, unexpectedly, I slide off Murdock's shoulder and fall in a heap on the ground.

There must be a hundred kids surrounding us by this time, with not a teacher in sight. Lonnie and Murdock are standing nose-to-nose, squared off. Murdock spits on Lonnie's shoes. "Yo' nothin' but a slave, you know that, Silver? Nothin' but a honkey-lovin' Uncle Tom."

Lonnie stands stone-like, his eyes fixed on Murdock. "Git," he says, "afore I knock your stupid head off."

The crowd gathers its collective breath; a new king of the playground has just been crowned. Not quite sure what he ought to do next, Murdock spins around and pushes his way through the crowd, leaving our astonished classmates with their mouths hanging open. Lonnie extends his hand to me and helps me up.

"Thanks," I say.

"Wasn't nothin'," he says, nonplussed. We walk up toward the school building together, and just as we reach the door the bell rings. I go in first and hold the door for Lonnie. "Thanks again, Lonnie," I say.

"Never mind," he answers. "Forget it."

But I don't forget. I have never forgotten.

That afternoon when school let out, I approached Lonnie with an idea that, quite frankly, I had never had the courage to bring up before then. I asked him if I could come over to his house some time. He smiled at the notion, and gave it a moment's thought. "Sure," he said. "You can do that someday."

"Why not today?" I asked. "It's Friday, and my mom won't care, as long as I call her and tell her where I am."

Lonnie looked over his shoulder nervously. "I'm gonna miss my bus," he said. "Check with me on Monday."

I was a little disappointed, but I understood. After all, I had sprung it on him impulsively. I would ask again on Monday. "Yeah, okay," I said. "Monday."

I was so excited at the prospect of getting to go over to the ever-popular Lonnie Silver's house, *in* Silvertown, no less, that I forgot all about the incident on the playground. I didn't even tell my parents what had happened. Instead, I told them I had been invited to go to Lonnie Silver's house. Lonnie Silver, of *the* Somerville Silver family.

"Are you sure that's a good idea?" my mother asked me.

"Well, sure," I said. "Everybody knows the Silver's, but Lonnie's *my* friend."

"Yes, sweetheart, I know," she said, "but let's just give it 'til Monday and see what happens, okay?"

I was puzzled by my mother's lack of enthusiasm, but then I figured, *she's just being Mom*. What I didn't know at the time, and didn't figure out until many years later after I had moved away, was that my mother knew why we never saw Lonnie or his family or any other black kids on weekends and holidays and such. I think in her mind she was trying to protect me, not from physical harm so much as psychological.

You see, like all the other kids at Mountain View, I had never thought anything of the fact that when we all got on our buses to go home, our bus went to our neighborhood, and Lonnie Silver, Stanley Murdock, and the other black kids got on a different bus that went to their neighborhood. To Silvertown. But Silvertown wasn't just another neighborhood like the ones we all went home to. Silvertown was the black section of town, full of rough dirt roads and shanty shacks. Ours was a segregated town. President Johnson had only recently signed the Civil Rights Act into law, and

Martin Luther King, Jr. hadn't told the nation about his dream yet. Blacks still couldn't go to the same restaurants whites could, or drink from the same water fountains as whites, Puerto Ricans, Italians, Jews, and everyone else.

    Mom knew this, of course, but I didn't. All I knew was that for a few short years Lonnie Silver was my friend. My *black* friend, yes, but I moved past that odd distinction the day he faced down Stanley Murdock and saved me from what was about to be an awful and humiliating beating at the hands of a future criminal in front of half the school. Lonnie didn't interfere because I was white and he felt sorry for me, or because he felt obligated. He squared off with Stanley Murdock because it was the right thing to do.

    I would like to believe that I became and stayed Lonnie's friend because he deemed me worthy of his friendship, and I his. Then again, considering the times, maybe we were each other's tokens. It's hard to know. In any case, I'm sad to say I never did go to Lonnie's house, or even to Silvertown, and neither he nor any other blacks ever came to my neighborhood.

    Imagine that.

LESSON 8

Heroes and Noogies

When I was in the fifth grade I had Mr. Harrison for the whole day, for every subject. That's how it was in the those days: you had one homeroom teacher for the entire day, for every subject, except maybe for music and gym classes. Mr. Harrison was tall, with very dark, closely cropped hair and deeply recessed, dull brown eyes. He must have been a first or second year teacher, because I remember he seemed young to me even then, and let's face it, when I was ten years old anybody over sixteen seemed like an adult. As far as I was concerned, all adults were from a faraway, hostile planet.

What made Mr. Harrison and fifth grade so remarkable in my school experience was that he was the first male teacher I had ever had. The first adult male I had ever seen at Wombat Elementary School. Until Mr. Harrison, the only adult males in my world had been my father, one grandfather, my uncles, and Stretch Griffith. Even my gym coaches and principal had been women. Suddenly, I was under the command of a fraternity brother, a guy who knew the emotional terrain of boyhood and understood why fart jokes and The Three Stooges were funny.

The unremarkable thing about Mr. Harrison was that he was a bland teacher. Nothing in my memory stands out about that year. Oh, I remember a few of the neighborhood kids who were in his class with me- Debbie King and Lily Rose come immediately to mind -and the evil Mr. Steele across the hall, who was a an emotional Sadist in his own right because he was renowned for his meanness, his black horn rimmed glasses, his scowl, and most important, his ability to nail a kid in the head with a chalk board eraser from across the room.

But no teacher in north central New Jersey struck fear in the hearts of fifth grade kids as much as the great and terrible sixth grade megalomaniac, Mr. Ross. From the moment I emerged from the cocoon of kindergarten into the bright sunlight of first grade and all through elementary school, I had heard stories about and shrunken from the awful reputation of Mr. Ross. Vlad the Impaler didn't have as frightening a reputation as Mr. Ross. Such were the legends of his temper and intolerance, not to mention the impossible academic demands he set before every cowering waif who ever had the misfortune of being assigned to his concentration camp of a classroom, that I sometimes stayed awake at night literally petrified with fear, knowing that someday my number was going to come up. It was inevitable. Someday I was going to have to face my awful, sickening destiny, I just knew it. I was not going to be one of the lucky ones whom the universe favored. I was not going to be able to avoid Mr. Ross the way our babysitter up the street, Tony Pelitierri, had had a strategy to avoid the draft by enlisting in the Navy before *his* number was called. I was a marked man, and I knew it.

In late May, the excitement and sadness of another school year ending, dovetailing into three glorious months of uninterrupted fantasies, baseball, beaches, and cool, green, shady afternoons under the trees along the banks of the Raritan River, made it easy to forget that besides report cards, I had one last hurdle to overcome before I was pardoned for Vacation Bible School and an interminable summer of long, hot, lazy days:

learning our fate for the fall. Traditionally, you found out on the final day of school who your sixth grade teacher was going to be in the fall. You knew going into the summer whether you had been condemned or spared. I needed to know: had the Grim Reaper of junior high school drawn my number? Or had I managed to beat the odds and dodge the dreaded, bloodthirsty tyrant Mr. Ross? On the last day of school I closed my eyes and crossed my fingers. I didn't eat breakfast and could barely eat my peanut butter and jelly sandwich at lunch. By the end of the day my vision was blurring and my stomach was queasy.

The anticipation was made even worse because our last report card was mailed home instead of handed out for us to take home and return signed the next day. That was where your fate was pronounced, at the bottom of your report card, in the fourth and last comments section: "Promoted to the 6th grade," and then . . . the name of the teacher who was to serve as your commander at the last academic outpost before you ventured into the narrow, ever-darkening valley of the shadow of adolescence. School ended on Tuesday that year; I wouldn't know my fate until at least the next day, possibly not until Thursday. The suspense was unbearable.

We all said our tearful goodbyes, and when the last kid in line had hugged Mr. Harrison, he instructed the class to gather the last of our crumpled papers, book reports, colored Social Studies maps, and every other piece of trash we had stuffed into the bowels of our desks and throw it away or take it all home.

"Mr. Harrison, what about this Tootsie Roll I found?"

"What about it, Jared?"

"I think it's been here since Halloween. Can I still eat it?"

"A Tootsie Roll? Are you kidding? That stuff'll outlast Styrofoam. Yes, you can eat it. By all means consume it. But eat it on the bus. And speaking of the bus, kids-" he checked the clock on the wall "-it's time to load the buses. Bye, everybody. Have a safe and happy summer."

With that, everyone cheered, and the class became a roomful of Mexican jumping beans trying to topple through a keyhole. Crowds of wild, cheering kids poured into the hallway like the Pamplona bull run: everyone scrambled for the back doors where just outside the fleet of dull yellow school buses sat in the sunshine with their windows down and their engines idling.

Free at last! Free at last! Thank God Almighty, we're free at last!

It wasn't until the bus dropped me off in front of my house that the full impact of summer and all that that implies hit me: no more stupid books about Johnny and Marianne trapped on Mystery Island, no more scratchy outdated movies about the sun and the planets, no more half-pint cartons of curdled cafeteria milk, no more Bruce Dertz putting me in a headlock on the playground and making me smell the B.O. in his armpits, no more insults from Deanie Savage. I dropped my book bag on the green grass and leaned against the decorative wooden slat fence that marked the corner of our front yard and waited for the sixth grade bus to drop off my next door neighbor and best friend Clark Fiedler and the other kids. The moment they stepped off the bus summer would officially begin.

The bus was late- sixth grade was held in a separate wing of the high school in those days because of overcrowding -and I was anxious. I couldn't wait to go throw a baseball and then start building that new underground fort in the woods Clark and I had been planning since Easter break. I picked up my book bag and ran inside to grab my baseball glove, and when I pushed through the screen door to go back outside, Clark's bus was just rolling up in front of my house, its alternating red lights flashing. Clark and the others spilled out like fire ants from a mound that's just been kicked, everybody laughing and screaming. That was when I heard it, my death sentence: Clark was leaping and hopping, shouting over and over, "You've got Ross! You've got Ross! Ha! Ha! Ha! You've got Ross!"

It was tradition- and I had completely forgotten this earlier in the day -for the sixth grade teachers to read the names of the incoming fifth graders who would be in their classes in the fall. Clark did not have Mr. Ross, but he had evidently risked life and limb to go to the Terrible One himself and ask if he would have me in his class in September, so powerful was Clark's need to get one up on me, to see me tortured at the hands of the murderous Count Ross.

In an instant my entire summer turned from bright blue sunny skies to ominous charcoal grey clouds; the brilliant sunshine was blotted out by the rain and gloom. My chest heaved and my hands turned clammy; my heart skipped at least a beat and a half, and I thought I might be having a heart attack. Clark, meanwhile, made an idiot of himself as he threw his book bag in the air and ran around the yard yelling jubilantly, "Ha! Ha! Ha! Johnson's got Ross! Johnson's got Ross!"

The summer dragged on, and I eventually forgot all about my autumnal fate. Mr. Ross did not haunt me at night, nor did I have trouble eating, screwing around with the felt board at Vacation Bible School to create my own more entertaining versions of the standard biblical stories, or anything else.

Summertime was the most supreme form of freedom that any kid could imagine, and life simply could not have been better.

Alas, all good things must come to an end, and so the summer came to a slow, uneventful close. Mom took David and me to Gaston's Department Store to get new clothes and school supplies, I was compelled to get a haircut and a comb, and against every fiber of my being I accepted the fact that summer was over. Soon I would meet the grim and detestable Mr. Ross for the first time, face-to-face.

I was already known for being something of a class clown, and friends who had had Mr. Ross the year before had undoubtedly tipped him off in May so that the minute he laid eyes on me he would have his red hot pinchers ready. Clark and the others, damn them, had set me up for even worse nightmares than I might have had if Mr. Ross had just been Mr. Ross and never known anything about me in advance. But now? I almost threw up in the back of the bus on the way to school.

It was bad enough that Ithe hand of Fate had cursed me to being in Mr. Ross's class, but the fact that our entire sixth grade group had to be on the Springwater High School campus with a thousand or more taunting, pimply teenagers only made the prospect of surviving Mr. Ross's class worse. At least we were somewhat isolated from the general population by being in our own wing. Even so, I shook with fear. I wanted to scream. I wanted to turn and run home and never set foot in any school again. But I couldn't; there was no way out. Instead, I ran into the boy's restroom, ducked into the farthest stall and slammed the door shut. I don't know what I was doing in there, maybe I thought if I stayed in the boys' room long enough the whole nightmare would go away.

After a while, though, kids stopped coming into the bathroom and I was left all alone. I knew it was time to face the inevitable and meet the dreaded Mr. Ross. I picked up my book bag and slinked out of the bathroom stall, half a step at a time. Out in the hallway, I crawled along the lockers toward my new classroom, the legendary chamber of horrors run by Mr. "I'm Going to Eat Your Still-Beating Heart While You Watch" Ross. Just outside his door I could see some of my fellow inmates moving about, getting situated in their assigned desks. Thankfully, Christopher Riglioni was one of them. At least I wasn't going to suffer alone.

I was taken aback when I first saw Mr. Ross; he wasn't at all what I had expected. I had expected a giant, a looming monster with wild hair and wild eyes. Instead, sitting behind his large wooden desk in the front of the room, his hands folded on the blotter in front of him, was a rather short, slightly built man with a very ruddy complexion, He looked as if he had been hanging upside down all morning. He had a stern expression on his face, and I noticed his hair was thinning and combed back, shiny but not greasy. He wore a brown tweed coat and a dark tie. Basically, he was an older, much smaller version of Mr. Harrison. He didn't look like a teacher you would want to cross, but he didn't have long yellow fangs dripping with blood either.

Mr. Ross either didn't notice or didn't mind that I was late- it was the first day of school, after all -so he told me my assigned seat between Christopher and some mouth breather I didn't know. When everyone was settled, Mr. Ross, rose and introduced himself, then led us in the Pledge of Allegiance. After that, he laid down the rules of engagement: *no* talking, *no* gum, *no* getting up out of your seat, *no* calling out, *no* late work, always raise your hand, heading in the upper right hand corner of every assignment. *That's an awful lot of "no's"*, I thought. But there were no threats, no explosions, no terroristic threats. Just business, all business. I knew then I was going to survive this guy after all. Just do what he said, and everything would be all right.

And so it went for the first weeks and months of school. Mr. Ross was indeed strict- he rarely joked or even broke a smile -but he was hardly the ferocious taskmaster we had all been led to believe he was. In fact, he was so predictable and effective as a teacher that I began to let my guard down and took advantage of those occasional moments when he too seemed to let his guard down, and I felt it was safe to venture into the entertainment field. When at last I felt the time was right, I would make a wisecrack or do something stupid like make an underarm fart sound- anything to get a laugh for my own amusement as well as the rest of the class. Mr. Ross was rarely amused, but he never attacked me, either. He threatened me all the time, and more than once he got that look on his face that male tigers get just before they eat their cubs, but most of the time one of his threats or that evil expression was enough to shut me down and put me back in my seat. In fact, I not only grew comfortable enough in his classroom to take the random, and later, the daily chance that I could slip something into the space and get a smile or a rise out of Mr. Ross, but I soon realized that I was learning more from him than I had ever learned from Mr. Harrison. Or Mrs. Davis; or Mrs. Baxter. I liked listening to Mr. Ross; I respected him, and yes, there was always that fear factor in the back of my mind. He may not have been the animal the older kids had warned me about, but he was no pushover, either. I had to be careful.

Eventually I crossed the line and got what was intended to be punishment, I suppose, though in my mind it was actually an honor. I fired off one smartass comment too many, so Mr. Ross made me move my desk to the front of the room and butt it up against his. He may have seen it as a punishment, but I saw it as a reward. Out of all the kids in his class, he had singled me out to come sit, literally, at his right hand. Other kids called out and made silly comments, too, but he didn't want them by his side. He wanted *me*.

Then the unthinkable happened. Sometime during the Christmas holiday, word came down through the grapevine, first to the parents, then to us, and finally to the local newspaper: Mr. Ross's brother and sister-in-law had been murdered. I never heard the particulars- I'm not sure anybody knew the details -but the story evolved that they had been victims of a home robbery, killed in their bed as they slept.

You can imagine that as an eleven, almost twelve year-old I had absolutely no idea how to react to such news. My parents, and the parents up and down our street, were in a somber mood for days after they heard. Mr. Ross did not return to school for two weeks after the holidays. Our class was subdued, even under the easy discipline of Mrs. Wilkis our substitute, and while no one said it out loud, we were all wondering the same things: Will Mr. Ross come back? What will we say to him? What *can* we say? Will he be the same Mr. Ross we've always known, or will he be different now?

On Monday morning, two weeks after we had first heard the news, I walked into Mr. Ross's classroom in the morning expecting to see Mrs. Wilkis as usual, and there he sat behind his desk, his hands folded as always, that familiar unreadable sour look on his face. He was staring out the window, as he often did while we were filing in. Our morning assignments were written on the chalkboard in his handwriting, just as they always had been and everything had the appearance of familiar routine. But there was tension in the air, you could feel it. Even a stranger would have known there was something wrong in the room. Like all the other kids, I sat still and quiet as a breath, waiting for Mr. Ross to rise and lead us in the Pledge of Allegiance.

A moment later he stood, and instinctively the class rose with him. As he had since the first day of school, he turned to face the flag, but this time instead of starting the pledge himself, he looked over his shoulder at me.

"Johnson, lead us in the pledge."

He always called me "Johnson." Had from the very first day. It was never "Heath" or "Mr. Johnson" or even a nickname, it was always "Johnson." And of this, for reasons I do not to this day know, I was immensely, immeasurably proud.

"I pledge allegiance to the flag of the United States of America," I recited, and Mr. Ross and the class spoke the words with me. I'm sure I wasn't the only kid in the class who felt a sense of relief because Mr. Ross had broken the ice. Moreover, he had handed the mantle to me, he had asked *me* to lead the class in the pledge and into normalcy. Whatever lonely painful world he had visited for the past two weeks was done with him and had sent him back to us. Perhaps reluctantly, perhaps fearfully, but he had entered our classroom to face the uncertain winds that the rest of the school year and the rest of his life were going to send his way.

Later that afternoon, I learned the most valuable lesson of my sixth grade year, and maybe in my entire school career. Mr.

Ross and I collided in a way that no man- including my own father -and I had ever run into one another before. He was in the middle of a lesson about Christopher Columbus, writing notes on the blackboard, when insanity took hold of my mind. Maybe I forgot myself in a moment of wistful longing, maybe Mr. Ross had done too good a job of letting the pressure out of the room so all of us could breathe again and try to return to the place we all needed to be. But in that moment when nothing but gas filled my head, I blurted out something about Chris's poor sense of direction and Puerto Rican sausages (Don't ask me what the connection was). There was a smattering of nervous laughter in the room, but I could tell the other kids were holding back, afraid of the genie I had just let out of the bottle. Suddenly, Mr. Ross stopped writing on the board mid-sentence, mid-thought, mid-everything, laid his piece of chalk down in the tray and, folding his arms authoritatively, turned around to level his sinister glare at me. A collective gasp hissed across the room.

"Johnson," he snarled, "do you have some information you'd like to add to the lesson? Something I neglected to mention?"

"N-no, sir."

"Come up here, boy."

Oh, man. Me and my big mouth. I hand't just crossed Mr. Ross's invisible line and entered his kill zone, but I had probably destroyed any good will and personal relationship I had had with this stern, amazing man. I glanced back at the class and saw that every eye was on me. I had a weak, sickening feeling in the pit of my stomach, and instantly regretted my own lack of self-control. I had just crapped all over my sixth grade teacher, a man I respected and who had made me love coming to school and love fighting for his attention because *his* attention meant more to me than anyone else's. I had ruined everything. And done it at the lowest point in his life. Now who was the horrible person?

"Let's go, Johnson, I don't have all day."

"Yes, sir." Ashamedly, I came around from behind my desk and walked up to him. I was almost as tall as he was; I could smell the Brylcreme in his hair.

"Right here," he commanded, pointing to a spot right next to him at the front of the room.

I fought back tears. "Yes, sir."

Slowly I walked up to the chalkboard where Mr. Ross stood waiting. When I reached him, he took the piece of chalk out of the tray and handed it to me.

"You see this space?" he said, indicating the open blackboard below his last line of notes.

"Yes, sir."

"I want you to write, 'I will not make fun of Christopher Columbus.'"

"Sir?"

"You heard me."

"Yes, sir." I took the chalk in hand and awkwardly wrote, *I will not make fun of Christopher Columbus.* When I finished, he held out his hand and took the chalk from me, then replaced it in the tray.

"Now turn around and face the class."

I did an embarrassing about face and looked out at the class, every one of them staring up at me as if they were about to witness an execution. The looks on their faces frightened me all the more.

"Johnson," said Mr. Ross, "have you been paying attention to a single word I've been saying?"

"Yes, sir."

"Good. Now, tell me. Did Christopher Columbus ever reach Puerto Rico?"

"No, sir."

"Well, then, what was that crack about Puerto Rican sausages?"

"I -I don't know, sir. I guess I was trying to be funny. Sometimes i just say things."

"Yes, you do."

I nodded sheepishly.

"Well, Johnson, I've got news for you." Suddenly, he wrapped his arm around my neck and pulled me into a soft but firm headlock. "Christopher Columbus didn't eat no steenkin' Puerto Rican sausages!" Then, with his other hand, he drilled his knuckle into the top of my head in one grand, crowd-pleasing noogie. The class howled.

"You hear me, Johnson?" he said, finishing the noogie and releasing me. "Columbus didn't eat sausage!"

"No, sir."

"He was a vegetarian."

Filled with surprise, wonder, and unrestricted relief, I looked into Mr. Ross's smiling face as he wrapped his arm around my neck a second time and pulled me to him. "Ya knucklehead," he said. "Now, go sit down."

I tried to let myself laugh with him and the class, but I couldn't, I just couldn't. My heart was broken. I felt as low and awful as I had ever felt in my life. This man, whom I had feared and dreaded, whose very name had struck me to the bone with terror before I had ever met him, had lost his brother and sister-in-law in the most horrible way imaginable. His grief was unfathomable. Yet, in his own inimitable Mr. Ross way, he had just told me, and demonstrated to the whole class, how much he loved me.

And, I guess, I had shown him how much I loved him, too.

LESSON 9

I Was A Spanish Speaking Crow

I didn't think much of myself when I was a kid, but one thing I was proud of was my sense of humor. By seventh grade I had established myself as a regular in the class clown rotation, with frequent appearances in both the principal's and guidance counselor's offices.

Our principal Mr. Dombrowski used to drum his fingers on his desk with an irked and confounded expression whenever I was sitting across from him in his office, the result of having pushed one too many envelopes in the classroom. "Mr. Johnson," he would say, "what exactly are your intentions here at Mountain View Junior High School?"

It was an excellent question, coming from such a clueless administrator, especially since I could never really explain it to him. I remember leaning forward one time, placing my elbows on the edge of his desk, and saying, "You know, Mr. Dombrowski, I've been wondering the same thing. A question like that requires a deep and thoughtful answer. But you know, after a great deal of time spent giving this matter my undivided attention, I think I've come up with an answer."

Mr. Dombrowski brightened and sat up taller in his leather swivel chair. "And that would be?"

"Well, sir, it's like this. I've come to the conclusion that this lovely little school of yours is a colossal bore. I've decided it's my civic duty to supply some entertainment."

Mr. Dombrowski sank back in his chair and let out a long, exasperated sigh. "You're a real smartass, aren't you, Johnson? You think you've got it all figured out, don't you?"

I leaned back in my chair, feeling smug. "No. Just this county lockup for morons."

**

I returned to school after three days' suspension, and was summoned to the guidance counselor's office before we had even said the morning pledge. With a disingenuous smile Mrs. Fleishman invited me to sit down on the white naugahyde couch across from her desk, her weighty perfume making it hard to breathe, and pulled up a chair next to me. I had only been in her office once before, and this being a return visit, I took a moment to look around again. She had the usual assortment of cheesy family portraits, a few numbskull inspirational posters, a fake plant on top of the file cabinet, and three inches of clutter on her desk.On the wall above and behind me hung a cheap painting of a gondolier navigating the murky canals of Venice. I assumed it was either a thinly veiled metaphor for junior high school, or a fantasy of what she would rather have been doing a that moment besides sitting in a cramped little office with me. She opened a file and, dabbing the tip of her thumb on her tongue every now and then, flipped through a stack of official-looking documents.

"What's all that?" I asked her.

"Your file," she said, without looking up.

"Anything interesting?"

"All of it," she said.

Life Lessons 101

**

The third week of September was a special time for the seventh graders at Mountain View, because that was when the teachers and counselors all huddled together and decided which kids were going to be placed in which level classes. Until then we'd all been assigned to classes more less by our last names and ages, and by our SRA standings at the end of sixth grade. We were really nothing more than junior high school recruits at boot camp, learning the rules, learning the basics, figuring out which teachers we should legitimately fear and which ones were young and gullible, or so close to retirement that they just didn't care anymore. But after three weeks of mutual reconnaissance, it was time for the brass to make their selections.

We had a three-tiered system at Mountain View: There were the eagles- they were the brainyacks, the "A-getters" we called them, the kids no one liked because they made the rest of us look stupid; the bluebirds- the kids who were definitely bright, maybe as bright as the eagles, but who weren't snobs or nerds; and the crows- everybody else. Along with being dubbed a certain specie of bird, a second layer of honor or humiliation was heaped upon every kid in the form of a foreign language. The eagles were placed in the French class, the bluebirds were assigned to take German, and the pigeons were dumped into the Spanish hopper.

Me llamo Paco.

Yep, I was a Spanish-speaking crow.

I wish I could say that being placed in the same holding tank with Bruno Kowalski, Jeb Phelps, Nadia Innes, Bruce Dertz, and the other intellectual lightweights who occupied the Top 40 slots on the popularity chart didn't bother me, but it did. In fact, it didn't just bother me, it incited me to new heights of rebellion.

First, I had gotten straight As and Bs until I hit the seventh grade. There were many reasons for my sudden fall from academic grace, among them my pre-algebra teacher Mrs. Picoult, a humorless raisin of a woman if ever there was one, or Mr. Dombrowski- whom I suspected was behind my demotion anyway -but in the end, it was my brain's fault.

See, in those days nobody knew anything about Attention Deficit Disorder or any of those other handy labels teachers and doctors apply to kids nowadays who ricochet off the walls because they know school is really nothing more than a weekly reminder that there's something worse than church. Back then was that if you couldn't sit still in your seat it meant you had a bladder problem; if you couldn't shut up while the teacher was talking it meant you were an incorrigible, rude showoff with insecurity issues; you were a poor reflection on your family. Worst of all, if you screwed up on tests or couldn't stay with a book because your mind filled up with so many exciting pictures and ideas that you couldn't decide which one to concentrate on, you were pegged as a dim bulb, or a fugitive from daycare. The thing was, I did all that stuff: I had great kidneys yet squirmed like a worm on a hook; I upstaged my teachers at every opportunity, yet I wasn't insecure at all. If anything, I was overconfident, and the only thing I ever quit was the Boy Scouts because I felt like a dork wearing a khaki uniform and struggling with that silly three finger salute. Besides, none of my friends were in the local troop.

Eventually, I figured out why I had been thrown overboard to swim with the bottom feeders: it was the team captain phenomenon. It didn't matter how many home runs I hit in baseball, or tackles I made on the football field, or how many times I ran the hundred yard dash faster than anybody in the school except for Kenny O'Donnell, I always got picked last, or close to it. It was the same thing in the classroom: it didn't matter how many "A"s I got on my essays, or how well I did on the Iowa Test of Basic Skills, or how many times I embarrassed that old bat Mrs. Lineal when she got her facts wrong in Social Studies. The team captains had chosen me last again.

A crow.

A flying garbage disposal.

Ése era yo.

LESSON 10

End Of The Night

What if a single day in a single year changed your life forever? What if three minutes out of twenty-four hours completely flipped your world, and you were never the same after that?

When I was in seventh grade I thought I knew how the world worked. Of all the things I understood best, other than rock and roll and how much I loved Sabrina Chavez, I understood that school was a prison with a liberal work release program. Our parents needed a place for us to put us during the day because they had no idea what to do with us when we were home, and the teachers didn't know what to do with us either. Between them it seemed the only thing they could come up with as to hold us hostage until we were old enough to figure out on our own what we wanted to do with our lives. I had a deep and abiding fear that by the time I figured out what I wanted to be when I grew up, I would already *be* grown up, and it would be too late to do anything about it.

Forcing a kid like me to wile away the hours of his youth in school day after day for no apparent reason is a dangerous proposition. You're asking for trouble. Instead of wasting away like incorrigible inmates in solitary confinement, kids like me get restless. We start thinking up ways to stir the soup. We ask questions. If you're going to force me to learn about American History and the founding fathers, make it worth my while and for heaven's sake. Tell me the *truth*. And while you're at it, tell me why I have to know any of this stuff at all. Better yet, how about a little practical information instead? How do you buy a car? What do I need to do to get a decent job? Why does my old man hate the Beatles and the Rolling Stones when he's never even heard their music? If there really was a Great Flood, where did all the water go? What, exactly is love anyway? And while we're on the subject, would you mind telling me why my girlfriend swore through tear-filled eyes she would always love me and then dumped me for Billy Higgins a week later? How do you open a checking account? How do you know when you're officially a grown-up? And why, after thousands of years of death and destruction, do we still have wars?

I longed for answers to these and a thousand other questions whose topics, let alone answers, weren't in any of the textbooks, or in my homework assignments, and never came up in class discussion or at the dinner table at home.

Then, one day, I was answered.

In those days at Mountain View Junior High School, every kid had to take choir. Band and art and shop were electives, and there was a thing called Glee Club, which was choir for the truly affected nerds, but choir- basic choir -was on the menu for everybody, regardless of whether you could carry a tune or not. I didn't mind it as much as the other kids did because it was a blow-off class, one less hour of the day I had to spend being tortured with subordinate clauses or the distributive property or listening to Mrs. Lambert go on and on about fulcrums and reflexive whatevers. At least, in choir I could have some fun. You didn't have to learn anything that mattered, and I could fake singing. As long as I showed up and didn't rob somebody at gunpoint I couldn't fail.

The irony was that I absolutely loved music and should have loved choir, but I didn't. Rock and roll was relatively new in those days, and even though we lived just outside of New York City, there weren't many radio stations that played it. WABC played Top 40, but that was about it, unless you had a radio capable of pulling in one of the two or three F.M. stations in the region, and even then, only one played what they called "album rock." That is, they would play extended versions of songs from albums instead of the two and a half minute edited versions you heard on A.M. radio. I listened to the radio constantly, and by the seventh grade I had managed to buy a handful of albums for myself, but only with a secret okay from my mother and a pact with her that we would not tell the old man about the albums until I was sixteen.

As I say, choir should have been a Sabrina for me, loving music as much as I did, but it was just the opposite. I thought it was a joke. Mrs. Laird tried her best to get us to appreciate the finer aspects of music, but she might as well have been trying to teach TV repair to a pack of hounds. Nobody cared, and nobody listened. For one thing, Mrs. Laird was a skinny little black lady who was about as far removed from cool as it was possible to be this side of your grandmother. For another, she took her subject far too seriously and was totally judgmental in her assessments of what we liked to listen to. She never called our music noise or claimed that the dog had crapped on the stereo- two enriching evaluative comments my old man frequently used to review my tastes in music -but she was nonetheless stern in her opinion that a well-rounded human being opened his mind and his ears to all kinds of music and did not confine himself to any one genre exclusively, as that would necessarily label him as ignorant and narrow-minded. I didn't quite know what she meant, but I knew I didn't want to be whatever it was she said I would be if I didn't listen to her stuff too.

So, while everyone else in the class was throwing paper wads, giving each other wedgies, and generally wreaking havoc while this poor woman was trying to teach us Broadway show tunes, or playing Vivaldi on the piano, I made an honest effort to get what she was talking about. The problem was, none of it grabbed me. My old man had tried the same thing at home, only he had beaten me and my brother about the ears with Benny Goodman and swing jazz all our lives, and instead of endearing us to his worldview of music, he had taught us to hate the clarinet more than Brussels sprouts. I hated the clarinet then, and I hate it now.

Well, this went on in choir day after day, month after month. Mrs. Laird would greet us pleasantly enough, distribute sheet music or a libretto to the class and then forge ahead, trying to persuade a class of certified motor heads that there was more to the world of music than The Grateful Dead and the British Invasion. I'm sad to report that even I, as open minded as I temporarily tried to be, soon fell off the wagon and tuned her out. It meant far more to me to impress the guys from my neighborhood with how loudly I could make farting sounds by cupping my hand under my armpit and flapping my wing than it did to discover the subtleties of cadence and melody, of tempo and harmony.

By late spring, I think even Mrs. Laird had decided it wasn't a hill worth dying on. She definitely took her foot off the gas, though she didn't give up on us completely. I recall coming in one day and noticing she had an album cover propped up on a bookstand on the table by her piano at the front of the room. With virtually no explanation, she started the record on the turntable and watched us to see how we would react. It was a classical piece, so naturally it was beyond my comprehension and had no immediate appeal, except that I recognized at once that the music was supposed to represent the photograph on the front of the album cover. The cover, which I found absolutely mesmerizing, was a full-sized photo of the Grand Canyon. I don't know why the picture captivated me the way it did, but it was the first time I ever made the connection between a photograph and music. The impact was minor, but it was also permanent: music and visuals were a powerful combination. It was the Grand Canyon Suite, and Mrs. Laird was trying to introduce us to the marriage of music and visual art. Unfortunately, the delicacies of her approach were no match for the butcheries of our indifference. It was truly a shame.

However one day in May- and I will never, ever forget this - Mrs. Laird greeted us with absolute silence as the forty or so of us flooded into her room and clamored up onto the risers, just as we had every day since September. Usually, she sat at her piano flipping through sheet music as we poured in, maybe played a few chords to try to get our attention, but not this time. This time she stood in the front of the room with her arms folded, looking as if she were a behaviorist surveying the group for potential candidates for a scientific experiment. On the table was another album cover, propped up just as the Grand Canyon Suite album had been a few weeks before. This album, though, had a dark cover with a young long-haired man on the front, bare-shouldered and looking for all the world like a youthful Dionysus, an unblemished version of one of the ancient Greek statues I had seen in my history book. Behind him, partially superimposed on top of one another in a diminishing line, as if they were materializing out of thin air, were three other young men. Across the top of the album cover were two words in a rolling, intriguing script: The Doors. I had no idea who The Doors were, and I didn't particularly care, but like the Grand Canyon picture, the album cover caught my eye.

Mrs. Laird said nothing- she didn't even take roll. When the bell rang and everybody was in, she reached across the table to set the tone arm of the phonograph on the record. Interestingly, she placed it in the middle of the record, not at the beginning. Immediately, the eeriest, most captivating music I had ever heard wafted out of the speaker of the record player. This was slow music, but it was nothing like a ballad or a love song, and it wasn't loud. It was mysterious and seductive, tender and creepy at the same time. Weird, wobbly organ and echoing, ethereal guitar . . . not the kind of music you'd want to hear late at night on an empty stretch of highway, or in a graveyard at midnight. Still, I listened carefully. This was unlike anything I had ever heard before, anywhere.

In a moment, a smoky baritone voice began to sing.

"Take the highway to the end of the night . . . take a journey to the bright midnight."

He sang slowly, deliberately.

". . . some are born to sweet delight, some are born to the endless night."

The endless night. My God, that was *me!*

But what was he singing about, taking the highway to the end of the night? To *"the bright midnight"*? What was that?

This wasn't about wanting to hold your hand, or ending the war, or Mr. Tambourine Man. This was eerie, otherworldly stuff. Bewitching. Music from the Twilight Zone. He was singing lyrics that no singer I had ever heard would have dreamed of singing because no one I knew or had ever heard was even *thinking* about what lay on the other side of death and midnight. No one was talking about being born to realms of *anything*. And what was a "realm" anyway? I had to know!

It didn't take me long to learn that the singer was Jim Morrison, and that Morrison was a beguiling, shadowy demigod in the world of rock and roll, and indeed, in the world at large. He was truly one of life's psychological gladiators, and instantly I wanted to be like him. I wanted to *write* like him, *think* like him. Explore the bizarre, reptilian world he inhabited.

And so at once I began scribbling words in the margins of my notebooks in class. When everyone else was writing down equations in pre-algebra, I was trying my hand at Jim Morrison-like lyrics and poetry. It became an obsession, to find the perfect phrase, to paint the strangest mental picture I could and make my reader wonder where I came from, and more important, where I was trying to take him.

I eventually bought every album The Doors recorded and memorized every word Jim Morrison ever wrote. I was transfixed. Words and their power meant everything to me. I wrote poems that were beautiful and poems that were dreadful, not poetry at all. I wrote my very first short story, "The Egg That Ate The Earth," a tongue-in-cheek science fiction piece, the following year in eighth grade, and from there I wrote story after story after story. I wrote novels.

Life Lessons 101

I wrote and I wrote and I wrote. I read. And I read and I read and I read. I explored the realms of bliss, and I found the highway to the end of the night.

As it happens, I'm on the side of the highway to the end of the night right now, writing this. On my way to the bright midnight.

LESSON 11

Why A Locker Skunk Runs

When I was twelve I was the second fastest runner at Mountain View Junior High School. You name it: the 100-meter dash, 100-meter low hurdles, 200 meter dash- any and all sprint distances Coach Rowen told me to run, I ran. Turned on the afterburners and flew like an F-16 down the track, leaving everyone slack-jawed and wondering how this short, thick white kid could be so fast.

Everyone except for Kenny O'Donnell, that is.

Sean White could stay within a few strides of me, and Sal Napolitano usually managed a winded and distant third, but neither of them ever beat me. And the rest of the runners? Fuggetaboutit. Only Kenny O'Donnell could outrun me, and even then he rarely beat me by more than a step or two. Of course, it didn't hurt that he was six-two and had the stride of a giraffe. I was five-five and built like a chimpanzee. In retrospect I think my stocky, lopsided build may have worked to my advantage. After all, I had something to prove. In sports, as in all of life, attitude is everything. At five-five I was used to looking up to most of the other boys and just about all the girls, too. Call it the Napoleon complex, but I was determined to prove my worth to the other kids. If I couldn't out-jump them in basketball, outmaneuver them in soccer, or run over them in football, then by God I was going to outrun them on the track. And because I was faster than everyone in he school but Kenny, I automatically ascended to the elite ranks in the eyes of the coaches and the other boys. Biggest, baddest, fastest or any combination of the three was the ticket to instant acceptance and popularity. Like any twelve-year-old, I craved acceptance.

Naturally, when it came to choosing sides for any team sport we played at school, on the playground, in gym class, or even in the neighborhood on the weekends, Kenny and Sean were inevitably named team captains. They were the alpha males in the subset of our junior high community, based solely upon their popularity, which was based, in turn, on their abilities to throw, hit and bounce balls. Valuable skills, to be sure, and skills I definitely possessed.

It took me several seasons of being cast aside to wallow in the pack of "everybody else" to finally catch onto the idea that a) I was never- *never* -going to be named a captain of anything, and b) that I was never going to be picked first for any team. Period. For the longest time I honestly believed that team captains were chosen based upon their superior athletic ability and leadership skills. It didn't matter that I could outrun Sean and give Kenny a hard chase every time Coach Rowan made us run, or that I could launch the ball higher and farther than anyone else in kickball, or even that I consistently hit home runs when other guys were whiffing or getting lucky dribblers past the infield in baseball. I was short and pale and freckled, so I wasn't popular. I took Spanish, not French or German, and when it came to the girls, I was anything but a heartthrob. I wasn't even an afterthought. So, like a flake of lint on a clean black shirt, I was cast aside in the pickup game draft, relegated to the crowd of unclaimed players on waivers, left to stand around clawing at the ground with my cleats like an antsy rooster, waiting for my name to be called.

In our neighborhood, it didn't matter which team you got on in the end, as long as you were taken high in the draft. The sooner you were picked, the more popular it meant you were and the higher your stud status in the herd. I don't know what kind of hallucinogens I was on at the time to have ever believed I would be picked anywhere but near the bottom, let alone near the top, but every time Kenny and Sean squared off to choose sides I expected to hear my name first. If the field was particularly strong on a given day- say, if a couple of the second team football players from the high school showed up and muscled their way into the lineups -I would have to face reality and accept the fact that my stock had instantly dropped, that there was no avoiding a slide down the ladder. Then, as the pool of players would begin to dwindle, and my hopes of gaining any sort of foothold in the cliffs of respect would diminish, disappointment would well up and fill me to overflowing, until I was so angry and hurt I wanted to cry. I'd grow increasingly frustrated, knowing that again- for the millionth time -I was going to have to prove myself to a bunch of blockheads whose IQs were about the same as standard tire pressure.

In the end, the only other kids left standing around waiting to be picked were the dorks and the chub monkeys. And me. I was a chub monkey, a dork. A dork who could hit home runs consistently, outrun everyone but Kenny O'Donnell, climb the rope higher and faster than anyone in gym class- *including* Kenny O'Donnell and Sean White. It was ridiculous.

I thought then, and I still think, that it really came down to trust. Kids, like adults, have a built-in trust meter they use on each other like body fat calipers. Unfortunately, kid trust has nothing to do with being truthful or honest or reliable. It has to do with *I'm counting on you to stand up for me no matter how big an ass I make of myself; I expect you to believe every word I say, no matter how wrong I am or how stupid I sound. I'll humiliate you in front of the whole school and fill your mouth with broken teeth if you ever talk behind my back.*

It was a never-ending struggle to win over the jocks and cool kids. Every once in a while I got momentary recognition when I lifted a fastball into Mrs. Greyson's garden, or slipped past 220-pound trash-talking all-state linebacker Alex Chevalier and ran 98 yards for the winning touchdown, but when the game was over I still wandered off the field alone, bruised and battered, wondering why I hadn't been invited to go the other direction with the big shots to grab a burger at Lou's Diner. I had to face the truth: I was born a locker skunk, and I was always going to be a locker skunk.

There was one event, ironically, where I found myself on equal footing with Kenny and Sean and all the rest of the popular guys: the infamous 600-yard "dash" around the soccer field. To a man, we despised Coach Rowan's weekly version of the Bataan Death March. There wasn't a kid in the school who could hold his head up high and say, "All *right*! 'Bout time we got to do something fun!" Least of all, Kenny O'Donnell. I was surprised to discover that guys like Kenny were dragsters, not Indy cars. They were good for a quarter of the distance and then they flamed out.

Trouble was, I rarely finished the 600-yard dash intact myself without having to walk long stretches of it. Apparently, I was a dragster, too. On the other hand, there was Clark Newdecker, a tall emaciated kid who looked as if he could climb through a keyhole and still have daylight on either side, who seemed to glide around the field effortlessly and cross the finish line without a bead of sweat on his brow and showing absolutely no signs of being winded. More important, Coach Rowan noticed Clark too, and always shouted Newdecker's time with a flourish. "Atta boy, Newdecker! Looka that boy fly! What a freakin' gazelle! A minute fifty-four, ya nutty nut!"

Then he would turn his dented fire engine red megaphone on us, the panting, loping throng, a full turn-and-a-half behind Clark. "What the heck's wrong with the rest of you girls? Why can't you be like Newdecker? C'mon, you bunch of pansies! *Move it! Move it! Move it!* White, you big can of lard, *turn* that corner; you're banking it! You look like a cement mixer on the clover leaf! Gruber, Pinkney, Jacks, you herd of hippos! You'll never shed the tonnage waddling like that! Kowalski! Jesus! You know, if you'd drop forty pounds you might finish by sundown! Come on, boys! Don't make me call an ambulance! Johnson! My *grandmother* can outrun you! You want me to get her walker for you, son? Lift those knees, boy! That's right, one foot in front of the other. One step, two step, three step . . . There you go! And your teachers said you couldn't learn!"

Like most of the others, I eventually trotted in, beyond exhausted, not caring whether I came in first, last, or in between. *Nobody* cared how he did in the 600 hundred yard dash, except Clark Newdecker.

It was after one of these debilitating runs that I hit on an idea: *What would happen if I ran the 600 yard dash faster than Clark Newdecker? What if no one could beat me? Would I get picked first then? Maybe even be captain?*

I started running around the neighborhood. Not fast, not far. But every day, rain or shine, hot or cold, snow or sunburn, I ran. Ran the neighborhood, ran past the Willis farm, down to Wombat Elementary School and back. Each day a little more time, a little more winded, but able to complete a distance I had envisioned and planned the night before. I had no way of knowing how far I was running- first, because I had no sense of time or distance, and second, because like time, half a measured mile seems so much farther to a kid than it actually is -but it didn't matter. All I knew was that the 600 yard dash was becoming child's play to me. I was out in front of the entire class every time out; I was even finishing ahead of Clarke Newdecker. Not by much, but ahead of him nonetheless.

By the autumn of my freshman year in high school, I could run farther than anybody at Springwater High School. Out of the blue, the cross country coach, Frank Cznewski, wanted me; Sabina Chavez and Laurie Pipkin were paying attention to me; and Kenny O'Donnell and Sean White were acknowledging me in the halls. I still wasn't "in" enough to eat at any of the cool lunch tables in the cafeteria, but running had provided me just enough status in the Springwater High School subculture to sidestep the ignominy generally reserved for the freaks and outcasts. I found a new lightness in my step, and a smidgeon more self-confidence, knowing that from now on I would be drafted higher- much higher - in the draft in any game where captains were designated to choose players for their teams.

But nothing changed. Softball, baseball, basketball, dodgeball, soccer, football . . . With only the rare exception- and that was when the captain was a jock who didn't know me -I remained a bottom dweller. I told myself it didn't matter, that it didn't bother me, though in truth it hurt a lot. Maybe Einstein and Napoleon and Harry Chapin were picked last too, but that didn't mean it didn't grieve them. Like me, they just learned to expect it, and they found creative ways of dealing with their lack of acceptance.

I kept on running throughout the rest of high school, but not for the cross country team or for any sanctioned track and field competitions. I ran for me. I ran when I felt like it, and I ran as far or as short a distance as I wanted to. Sadly, my attitude toward running quickly devolved from key to acceptance to necessary chore.

After high school, life caught up with me and I stopped running altogether. I took up lifting weights in the gym, and I was active outdoors, but if I ran at all, I ran only as a way to maintain my muscle tone. I hated the very idea of running. For years, after learning the painful lesson that excelling at a sport- or at anything -is no guarantee of peer acceptance or popularity, I scoffed at those who tried to wedge their way into social circles that had no intention of, and not even a mechanism for, letting them in.

Flash forward: about three years ago I picked up running again. I'm not sure why; maybe it was because I saw so many guys my age and younger turning to flabby candles, and I didn't want that to happen to me. Maybe it was the competitor in me, or I was just plain jealous. Who knows? I had never run farther than seven miles in my life, and *that* only once. But I ran on, and on, and on, and only a year after starting from scratch I ran my first half marathon. That's 13.1 miles. The experience gave me such a high that ten minutes after it was over I decided I had to do it again. It also gave me pause to seriously question my own sanity. Nevertheless, four months later I ran another half marathon. Six months after *that*, I ran a full marathon, 26.2 miles, in Washington, D.C.

But here's the thing: I don't play baseball or hit home runs anymore; I don't play football or try to outrun guys twice my size. I can only hit the long range jump shot if the wind is behind me and the gods are smiling. I'm still picked last on any team; the teachers I work with still won't ask me to join them at their lunch tables, and the only time I sprint these days is to the bathroom.

The cool thing, though, is that I never win a race I run, and yet I always receive a winner's medal. Everybody who knows I run long distances, no matter how little or how much time I take to finish, admires and respects me. And of the jocks and cool dudes who wouldn't pick me for their teams? Well, nowadays, if they need to cover 13.1 miles, or 26.2 miles, or even 600 yards, they climb in their cars and drive it.

LESSON 12

A Slave To Fashion

When I was in the seventh grade- this would have been 1967, in the spring before the famous Summer of Love -a new boy enrolled at Mountain View Junior High. He seemed to come from out of nowhere. On Monday he was as invisible and unknown to any of us as the breezes in China, and by Wednesday everyone in the school knew his name and where he was from. His name was Grant Walsh, and he was from Columbus, Georgia.

Grant had wavy blonde hair and striking blue eyes that offset his olive skin. He was average height, built like a baseball player, and had a maddening genteel southern lilt to his voice that made the girls swoon and the boys want to stuff him in his locker. Above all, he was an impeccable dresser. While most of the boys were dressing to imitate the Beatles or the Grateful Dead, Grant was dressing like a model as if he had just stepped out of fashion magazine. He wore blue jeans like the rest of us, but while we wore tie dye tee shirts or, in the case of the greasers, plain undershirts, he wore crisply ironed button down shirts- *with collars* -and freshly shined penny loafers. It was really despicable.

The boys all hated Grant because the girls all loved him. He was perfect. Perfect hair, perfect teeth, perfect manicure, perfect grades, a talented musician, gifted athlete . . . and that cutesy little southern accent that contrasted so vibrantly against the oily dialects of the north central New Jersey locals; it made all of us feel grimy and uneducated. We hated Grant because he was better than we were; we envied him because he was everything all of us other boys, until Grant appeared on the scene, only imagined ourselves to be.

Like all the other boys at Mountain View, I couldn't stand Grant at first. It was hard enough for me to make any sort of impression on the girls as it was. I wasn't popular, wasn't confident, wasn't good-looking, and wasn't on any of the sports teams. I was a harmless and only marginally rebellious thirteen-year-old kid trying to stand out in a crowd of street thugs, future car mechanics, and illegitimate sons of Mafia hit men. What chance did I have against Grant Walsh, Mr. Perfect?

For the rest of that fall the pressure of trying to measure up to Grant Walsh was almost unbearable. Those who were up to the challenge did everything they could to work their way into his inner circle so that at the very least they could be *seen* with him, if not actually be like him. Those who couldn't keep up- or who refused to even try -were left in the social dust, fashion buzzards hanging around on the fringes of Mountain View Junior High School, expecting someone on the inside to weaken and fall out, yet knowing it was never going to happen.

That put the pressure squarely on me. I had to make a decision. Do I maintain my lonely, essentially invisible (but familiar) orbit among the socially insignificant, or do I succumb and adapt in the dubious hope that by following Grant's example I might gain some traction and move into the fast lane?

Self-respect and a genuine loathing toward Grant Walsh gave me the answer right away: screw the Georgia peach and his ridiculous costumes. I was gonna stand on my own; I was gonna set my own trends.

Uh-huh. Until I realized that not only was I not gaining any ground with the girls by being "true unto mine own self," I was watching Grant pick up speed, every one of the girls and most of the boys drafting behind him. I had to do something, or I was going to doom myself to permanent romantic oblivion. So, one day, I made what was to me a monumental and gut wrenching decision. I sold out. Abandoned every principle I had ever believed in, disavowed every protesting, anti-follow-the-crowd word I had ever uttered: I decided to copy Grant. I hated myself for even *considering* imitating that phony, grits-eating Georgia pretty boy. But he was winning the war. Heck, he was *running* it. I told myself I wasn't one of the sheep; I was doing what I had to survive.

As it happened, the next trend Grant started was Dickies. A very fashionable accessory at the time that had evolved from the casual look of the folk music scene in the early 60s, and an inevitable response to the berets and Bohemian poetry slam clothes the Beatniks wore in the 50s, a Dickie was nothing more than a turtle neck collar attached to two short flaps of knitted material that you slipped over your head and wore a shirt over so that it looked like you had a full turtleneck sweater on underneath, but you really didn't. It was the sweater equivalent of a clip-on tie. Naturally, Grant had caught onto it before the rest of us.

The first time Grant came to school wearing a Dickie, he wore an outfit that consisted of sharply creased blue jeans, black dress socks, black loafers, a white button-down shirt with blue pinstripes, and a black Dickie. Naturally, the blue pinstripes and jeans were designed to offset Grant's sapphire blue eyes, and the white of his shirt highlighted his perfectly combed blonde hair. He looked amazing. And don't believe for a second that every kid in the school didn't take immediate and serious note of what he was wearing, including me.

I went home that afternoon and told my mother what Grant had worn to school that day, and insisted she take me to Gaston's Department Store to buy me a Dickie.

"I'm not going to drop everything and drive you down to the store just so you can look like Grant whats-his-name," she said, peeling potatoes over the kitchen sink.

"But you don't understand," I pleaded. "Everybody looks at Grant, especially the girls. All I want to do is keep up with what's fashionable, that's all."

"You want to look like Grant, in other words," she said, plopping the raw potatoes in a pot of water on the stove.

"No, I don't," I protested. "Dickies are a groovy look. It's what everyone is wearing these days."

"Oh. So you want to look like everyone else," Mom said. She reached into the refrigerator and took out a bundle of carrots. "What happened to being independent? I thought you *didn't* want to look or be like everyone else."

"Well . . . I don't," I said. "It's just- it's just that Dickies are a groovy look."

She pulled the rubber band off of the carrots, placed them on her wooden cutting board, and then topped them with a pairing knife. "I'm confused," she said. "You want to look like Grant whats-his-name, but you don't want to look like Grant whats-his-name."

"Walsh."

"Fine. Walsh. You want to be independent and do your own thing, but you want to wear what everyone else is wearing."

"No, you don't understand."

She took a thick, bright orange carrot in her left hand and ran the peeler along its length as she rotated it in her hand. "Oh, I understand, all right. You want to be fashionable so the girls will notice you. You think that if you dress like Grant whats-his-name . . . Walsh . . . then everyone will like you the way they like him. Right?"

"Yes! I mean, no. I mean-"

"Do you and Grant look alike?"

"No."

"And you say he's from Georgia?"

"Yes."

"Mmm. I'll bet he's got that charming southern accent, doesn't he?"

"If you mean, does he sound like a hillbilly, then yeah, he's got an accent."

"So if you don't look anything like him, and you don't sound anything like him, how is dressing like him going to change how people see you?"

"Mom, can we just go get me a Dickie? *Please?* I don't want a lecture."

She checked the clock on the wall and wiped her hands on her apron as she untied it from around her waist. "I swear, you're going to be the death of me. Okay, let's go. We have just enough time to make it and get back before your father comes home for dinner. But remember, this is coming out of your allowance, young man."

"Okay, okay. Can we go now?"

With exasperation in her tone and on her face, Mom grabbed her purse and car keys and drove me down to Gaston's. To her surprise (and quite honestly, to mine also) there was a whole display devoted to Dickies in the Men and Boys section of the store, between the slacks and dress shirts. I chose a deep dark brown Dickie- earth colors suited my hair and personality best -and my mother paid for it with a check. I couldn't wait to get home and try it on.

As soon as we were home, Mom went back to making dinner and I dashed upstairs to my bedroom to begin trying on shirts over my new Dickie. I hadn't tried on the Dickie at the store, and now when I slipped it over my head it felt a little tight around my throat; truth be told, it was a squeeze. Not comfortable at all. No matter; it would loosen up with wearings. I grabbed a handful of shirts out of my closet and one by one tried them on over the Dickie, but none of them made me look even remotely like Grant Walsh. I tried every combination I could think of, but nothing worked. I had planned to wear my new look to school the next day, so I was going to have to find a combination that came close to the look I was searching for. Finally, I settled for a solid white button-down shirt, my best pair of jeans, and my cleanest pair of Keds sneakers (I didn't have loafers yet). Just before Mom called me down for dinner I tried on the entire outfit and admired myself in the bathroom mirror.

"What are you doing?" David, who was standing in the doorway, asked,

"Trying on my new look," I said.

"New look? What new look? You're just as ugly as you were this morning."

"Dry up and blow away," I said.

David skipped down the stairs, laughing hysterically. "Hey, Mom!" he hollered. "Heath looks like Ken!"

"Who?" I heard my dad call from the living room.

"Ken. Barbie and Ken!" David yelled, loudly enough that I would be sure to hear him.

"Oh," said the old man. "Who are Barbie and Ken?"

The next day I went to school in my new outfit feeling for all the world like a movie star. The wool knit collar of the Dickie scratched and choked my throat, but I couldn't wait for everyone, especially the girls- especially Sabrina Chavez -to turn their heads and admire me. It was going to be worth a little discomfort. Now I knew what stupid old Grant Walsh went through every day just to look sharp.

Stupid. There's the key word. Not only did almost no one notice anything different about me all day- and the few who did made comments such as, "Trying to look like Grant, are you, Johnson?" -but I felt stupid. As though I were impersonating someone else; as though I were trying to be someone or something I wasn't. The Dickie was stiff and and made it hard to breathe. I had to watch how I sat and walked so I wouldn't undo my carefully tucked-in shirt or ruffle the flaps of my Dickie. God forbid if it bunched up and made me look as though I had a roll of hot dogs under my shirt.

I could not have been more disappointed that day. I thought wearing a Dickie would make a difference, but it didn't. Mercifully, Grant only stuck with the look for about a week and a half, so when he quit it, so did I- and the handful of other boys who had tried the look, too.

I don't remember what the next few trends were that Grant introduced us to, but I remember one I thought was unusually corny, even for Grant. He twisted his belt 90 degrees to the left, so that the buckle rested over his left hip. *How dumb*, I thought. *How are you supposed to get your pants off if you have to . . . you know?* Still, dumb as I thought it was, I twisted my belt around too the next day. So did most of the other boys, I noticed. Anything for love and recognition.

In the weeks and months that followed, I imitated each of Grant's fashion quirks in its turn, always with the same results. The other boys all teased me about trying to be like Grant, and the girls still looked right through me. I was invisible. Nonetheless, I persevered. I was on a mission, and I figured it was only a matter of time before I scored a look that would not only put me on the same playing field as Grant Walsh, but would draw the attention of the girls, especially, I hoped, Sabrina Chavez.

It was in the spring that Grant pulled his coup de-grâce. One Monday morning, he came in with nothing new on. Absolutely nothing. I was completely taken aback, wondering what was going on. He didn't have s single new piece of apparel on him. In fact, I recognized the jeans, the shirt and the shoes. *Hey, what gives?* I wondered. His hair wasn't even combed. No one said anything, but I could tell by the way they were staring at him that they noticed the change in Grant just as I did. I didn't know about the others, but my guess was that he was up to something. It was always possible he had had a fight with his mother and she had made him wear normal clothes in the normal way as punishment, but I had my doubts. Grant was too charming for that to be the explanation. I figured he was just having an off day and would be back in school the next day with some new gimmick, and like fools the rest of us would follow whatever ridiculous trend he started.

But on Tuesday, Grant came to school in familiar and ordinary clothes again, things we had seen before. No Dickie. No sideways belt. No Apache tie. No Nehru jacket. Just ordinary, everyday junior high school kid clothes.

This went on day after day after day. For whatever reason, Grant had abdicated the throne. Maybe he had tired of the pressure of being a trend setter. He was only human, after all.

"I don't get it," I said to Mom one evening while she was stirring her world famous spaghetti sauce in a huge pot on the stove.

"What don't you get?" she asked. She offered me the spoon to taste the sauce.

"Grant Walsh. He started this whole fashion thing when he first transferred to school, right?"

"Mm-hmm. Dickies. Apache ties. Looking groovy. Yes, I remember. Did it ever help you with the girls?"

"Not exactly. Sabrina Chavez still doesn't know who I am."

"I'm sorry."

"Yeah, me too. But here's the thing. A couple of weeks ago Grant just stopped."

"Stopped what?"

"Wearing new stuff. I mean, one day he just quit. He came to school like the rest of us, and he's been doing it ever since."

Mom dumped a couple of wads of stiff pasta into a large pot of boiling water. "Oh my. I'll bet the girls all turned on him, didn't they?"

"No, that's just it. They didn't. And the guys didn't, either. He's as popular as ever."

"So what do you think that means?"

"I'm not sure. But I think we wasted a lot of money on stuff I didn't need."

Mom smiled.

"You know, it's kind of funny," she mused.

"What's that?"

"Well, fashion usually comes out of New York or Paris or Italy- someplace like that, right?"

"I guess."

"Then how is it a slick little southern boy from Georgia was leading you boys by the nose? I mean, shouldn't he be following you? You're the sophisticated northern boys, after all. Did he ever tell you to follow him?"

"No. We just did."

Mom smiled again. "Imagine that. Well, go upstairs and tell your brother it's time for dinner, will you?"

LESSON 13

Extra Hair Versus Mustache and Fingernails

The big reward for every kid in the eighth grade at Mountain View Junior High School was a three day, two night class trip to Washington, D.C. No matter what part of town you lived in, no matter how high or low your grades were, no matter how many times the teachers offered you adoption papers or stuck pins in a voodoo doll of you, if you were a member of the graduating eighth grade class at Mountain View, you got to go to Washington, D.C. It was the administration and faculty's way of saying *thank you* to all the robins- the "A-getters" who had made the teachers look so much better than they actually were -and *good riddance* to the crows, those of us who had forced blood, sweat, and tears from the crappy teachers' brows and formed everlasting bonds with the best ones, often in spite of ourselves.

Truth be told, the Washington trip was the only reason half of us went to school in the spring. Like seniors in high school and college, eighth graders have essentially clocked out by spring break and have their eyes set on summer and whatever vague future lies on the other side of Labor Day. The very idea of a caravan of chartered Greyhound buses rolling down the interstate with three hundred fifty adolescents to take over a motel in the nation's capital for a full weekend two hundred miles away from home had all the signs and symptoms of a massive rock and roll tour. And don't think we didn't know it. All we talked about was how boys were going to sneak into the girls' rooms or sneak out of the motel entirely, who was going to pull what prank on whom, how we could smuggle in contraband, and how we were going to trash our rooms the way we had read Led Zeppelin and the Who did on *their* tours. Oh, sure, there was the prospect of visiting the Treasury, the White House, the Smithsonian Institute, Arlington National Cemetery, the Capitol, the F.B.I. Building, and the National Archives to glance at the Declaration of Independence and the Constitution- the Social Studies teachers had made sure we understood this was an educational tour -but only the nerds cared about those things. Until we gazed on those so-called national treasures in person, they were simply ideas we had taken notes on in class and taken tests over.

The catch if you wanted to go on the trip was that you had to avoid suspension all the way through seventh and eighth grade at Mountain View, and you had to have passed all of your classes. That was a tall order for some of the guys I hung around with, but not me. To spend three whole days away from my parents- which was as close to absolute freedom as I was going to get before I graduated high school -not to mention the chance to see Melinda Swanson and Sabrina Chavez in their bikinis in the motel pool, I would have eaten broken glass and walked across burning coals in my bare feet.

From the time we returned to school after Christmas break, the D.C. trip was all I thought about. I couldn't wait for the end of May to come. When my mother wrote the check for my trip payment and I handed it in to my homeroom teacher, I might as well have been sealing my reservation to the French Riviera. This was gonna be great!

There was just one catch. Mr. Lowenstein, Mountain View's wood and metal shop teacher, was the chaperone assigned to my bus. Ernst Blofeld wasn't out to get James Bond as much as Daniel Lowenstein was out to get me. Oh sure, there would be a couple of parent chaperones on each bus as well, but only one eighth grade teacher. We didn't care who the parents were, though, because we knew they weren't going to want to deal with us, and we had no intention of listening to anything a parent said anyway. Heck, you didn't do what your own parents told you to, so what made anybody think you'd do what somebody else's parent told you to do? Teachers were a different story, though, especially Mr. Lowenstein.

Mr. Lowenstein was a slight and ugly man who reminded me of a rodent. He had long dirty fingernails and always smelled of pine resin and flux. He wore the same old dusty blue denim jumpsuit every day and a dark, paint-encrusted canvas smock that hadn't been washed since the day the school opened. His face had been chiseled out of pasty clay and tapered to a dull point at his chin, with his ample white nose serving as an unavoidable reminder that ugly is forever. Whenever he was instructing the class about how to use the lathe or the table saw, or how to apply flux when you were fiberglassing, he'd constantly comb his greasy cowlick with his fingers to get the sawdust out of his hair, and flurries of tiny wood shavings would float to the floor like suicidal snowflakes.

So one day I was walking out of the tool room trying to figure out which end of the impact wrench in my hand was the business end, when Mr. Lowenstein intercepted me. "C'mere a minute, Johnson," he said. Why was it teachers were always calling me by my last name, never my first? "We need to talk," he said. He guided me over to a shadowed corner of the shop where the scrap lumber barrels were, looked me square in the eyes, and said, "You're on my bus for the Washington, D.C. trip, did you know that?"

"Yeah, I know," I said.

"Well, here's a newsflash for you," he said. "I'm not going to let you on my bus unless you get that mop cut."

I should mention that in 1968 not many boys were sporting long hair at Mountain View Junior High School. I may not have been the only one, but I know there weren't more than four or five of us. By today's standards my hair wasn't that long, just a little bit past the bottoms of my ears, but in those days that was plenty long enough to get yourself singled out and called "faggot" or "queer" by just about anybody with a set of lungs and a big mouth, and that included teachers.

"Why?" I asked.

"Because you look like a girl, that's why," he said. "All you need is a dress. Now, go get a haircut."

"I don't want to," I said.

"Okay, let me put it to you this way. If you don't get a haircut, you're not ridin' on my bus, and if you ain't on my bus, you ain't going to D.C. You savvy?"

"You can't make me get a haircut," I said.

"The hell I can't."

"Hey! You just cussed! Teachers can't cuss."

"The *hell* they can't."

"I'm telling Mr. Dombrowski and get you fired."

"Oh, yeah, Johnson. He'll believe *you*."

Dombrowski. Listen to me. What a joke. The only grownup at Mountain View Junior High School who hated me more than Mr. Lowenstein was Mr. Dombrowski. The front office, led by Heir Dombrowski, was an unfriendly members-only club who ordered take-out for lunch every day and took over an hour to eat while we kids had to wolf down stale sandwiches, soggy chips, and warm soda in fifteen minutes. As far as we could tell, not even the teachers had access to the secret chamber of Dombrowski's office unless they were in trouble, were one of his hand-picked enforcement goons, or were young and pretty, fresh out of college. Mr. Lowenstein was one of Dombrowski's enforcement goons. Everyone knew that Mr. Lowenstein could rob you at gunpoint in front of a hundred students and if you were one of Mr. Dombrowski's special discipline projects he would take Lowenstein's side and attack you like a piranha on a small pig. I was being railroaded, but there didn't seem to be much I could do about it. Not at the moment, at least. Even so, I was determined to stand my ground or go down fighting.

"What have you got against long hair?" I said.

"I told you, you look like a sissy. Now, when and if you decide you want to look like a boy, I suggest you start by getting a haircut. Otherwise, stay home while we're in Washington. I don't care which one you do. In the meantime, I've got a class to run." He cupped his hands on either side of his mouth trying to make himself heard over the noise of the shop and bellowed. "EVERYBODY CLEAN UP! Let's go! Ya got five minutes to the bell."

I was furious. All afternoon I ran Mr. Lowenstein's words through my mind, over and over: "you look like a girl"; "get a haircut"; "you ain't going to D.C." And the whole time I was steaming over what he said, I kept visualizing him raking his greasy hair over with his long yellow fingernails, flecks of sawdust coating his shoulders like dandruff, twitching his wiry, caked mustache, little knots of boogers in his nose . . .

Hey, wait a minute! Greasy hair. Filthy fingernails. Scraggly mustache. All at once I recognized Lowenstein's hypocrisy. Even Dombrowski wouldn't be able to hold off my argument! That slob Lowenstein was trying to boot me off his bus when I was at least three steps ahead of him when it came to personal hygiene. I could hardy wait for the chance to stick it to those two sanctimonious phonies. But I'd need help. Even though I was willing to fight the battle alone, I knew I stood a better chance of winning if I recruited some muscle.

"Hey, Mom, how'd you like to come to school with me tomorrow?"

I told my mother what was going on (the old man was out of town on a business trip), and the next morning she and I were in Mr. Dombrowski's office, along with Mr. Lowenstein, pleading my case before either of them had had his first cup of coffee. If Lowenstein could have dirty hair speckled with sawdust, pick his crusty nose with long fingernails, and grow a crooked mustache that looked as though something crawled out of his nose and lay across his upper lip to die, and he could still be in charge of a bus full of eighth graders going to Washington, D. C., I could have long clean hair and ride that bus.

Mr. Dombrowski never took his eyes off me the whole time he, Lowenstein, and my mother were talking. I was sure he was trying to figure a way to kill me, dispose of my body, and blame it on Lowenstein. But in the end he simply scratched the side of his nose and frowned at Mr. Lowenstein.

"Daniel, did you really say a cuss word in front of Mr. Johnson here?"

Mr. Lowenstein stiffened, looking offended at the very idea that he would use inappropriate language in the presence of one of his young charges. "Absolutely not," he huffed.

Mr. Dombrowski looked at me. "He says he didn't, Johnson, and I believe him."

"He said you'd say that," I sulked.

"Mr. Dombrowski," said my mother, "whether or not Mr. Lowenstein used foul language in front of my son is beside the point, although it certainly would be in keeping with his character. Here are the facts: My son wants to go to Washington, D.C. with his friends as part of the eighth grade celebration. I have paid for him to go. He has met all the school's stated and written requirements for eligibility. Therefore, there is no reason why he shouldn't go."

"But his hair, Mrs. Johnson . . ."

"What about his hair? It's clean, it's combed. That's more than I can say for his teacher."

Mom had him there. Turning to face me and Mr. Lowenstein simultaneously, she shot a quick glance at Dombrowski to make sure he was paying close attention. "Hold out your hands," she ordered Lowenstein and me. I held out my hands, but Mr. Lowenstein refused.

"I have no intention of holding my hands out just because you say so," he protested.

"Do it!" she insisted.

Sheepishly, Mr. Lowenstein held out his hands. It was like comparing Palm Springs to Beirut. "Do you see that, Mr. Dombrowski? And this man has the audacity to refuse my son on his bus. If you ask me, it should be the other way around. This little rodent needs to do some cleaning up of his own, don't you think?"

At that, I was invited to leave Mr. Dombrowski's office, which I was more than happy to do, but I stuck around outside across from his secretary Mrs. Schlemp's desk listening as best I could to the melee going on inside. Unfortunately, I could only make out the occasional phrase or word, but when Mr. Dombrowski opened the door a few minutes later to let my mother out, I knew how the skirmish had gone. Mom was smiling, and Mr. Lowenstein looked as though he had just watched an eighteen wheeler back over his brand new Corvette. It wasn't a pretty sight.

But Washington, D.C. sure was.

LESSON 14

8th Grade: You Are Here

Eighth grade was the gateway to all things forbidden and free when I was a kid. Too big to even be called a kid, I was actually stuck in that purgatorial zone known as junior high school, where no one on your street, in your town, or even on the planet knows you're alive, except your teachers and your parents- and as often as not, *they* secretly wish you would be spirited away by aliens for the balance of your teenage years and then returned when you're twenty-five and over yourself. The problem was that I didn't know at the time just how much I didn't know. All I knew was that high school was right in front of me. I was a minor league ball player about to break into the Big Leagues and make history.

Face it: there's no talking to an eighth grader. Rational discourse? Forget it. You're a moron; you don't know what you're talking about.

Consequences? What consequences? *They're never going to catch me; I've thought of everything.*

The future? Open your eyes before you run into it. *Hey, mom! When's lunch?*

Common sense? A myth. *No, mom, I don't need a coat; Jesus, it's only fourteen below!*

Maturity? Another myth. *God, you treat me like such a baby! I know I'm supposed to put my underwear in the hamper!*

Thus, presented with incontrovertible evidence that I, as a worldly and sophisticated 14-year-old, was shackled to a pair of idiots for parents and was legally forced to spend nine months of my life each calendar year, five days a week, eight hours a day, with fools who knew absolutely nothing about me or my world, I rebelled. I skipped class. I played hooky. I slouched and doodled and slept and played the fool for a captive and generally appreciative audience. Thanks to a testosterone-fueled ego, James Bond movies, and a host of other social influences including rock and roll and miniskirts, I was the ubiquitous, all-knowing, all-seeing teenager with all the answers. That is, until I was sitting in the guidance counselor's office one day in the spring of my eighth grade year. Mrs. Spielhoffer was going over the list of course options for my freshman year in the fall at Lakeshore Castle High School, which of course wasn't registering in my head at all because a) it was boring, and b) I was in love with Sabrina Chavez, who at the time happened to be sitting in the waiting area on the other side of the glass to Mrs. Spielhoffer's office.

So as Mrs. Spielhoffer prattled on about credits and graduation requirements, I daydreamed about Sabrina. Then, seemingly out of nowhere, I heard the word "graduation," and as if I'd been launched from a catapult, I honed in on Mrs. Spielhoffer and the papers spread out on her desk in front of me.

"I'm sorry," I said. "Would you go over that again?"

Mrs. Spielhoffer let out an exasperated sigh and ran the point of her pencil to the bottom of the course list. "I said, once you graduate, you have all kinds of options about what you want to do with the rest of your life. There's college, foreign service, the Peace Corps, the military-"

"Military!" I gasped. "I don't want to go to Vietnam."

"Well, I didn't say you did. I'm just pointing out that once you're finished with high school, everything becomes optional. You can choose to continue your education, or you can do something else. It's all up to you. You see, once you have your diploma, you're not required to go to school anymore."

"Yeah?"

"Mm-hmm. Of course, you'll have to do something else, as I say. You can't live at home for the rest of your life."

And that was when it hit me. *I'm not ready to be on my own. I'll* never *be ready!*

I was in a daze for the next fifteen minutes as Mrs. Spielhoffer selected my freshman courses for me and then had me sign off on my fall schedule. My mind was buzzing. I didn't so much as glance at Sabrina on my way out of Mrs. Spielhoffer's office. I returned to Social Studies, collapsed in my seat, and stared off into space dazed and confused, a scared little rabbit. I opened my notebook to a blank page and drew a horizontal line with a "K" on the left side and a "12" on the other. Two-thirds to the right of the "K" I drew a short vertical line and wrote the number "8" above it. Then I drew a small curved arrow pointing to the "8" and scribbled "You are here."

My thoughts raced around inside my head, chasing and crashing into each other; my breathing became labored. *Jesus,* I thought. *I don't know* anything*!*

Here I was in eighth grade, two-thirds of the way through all the formal education I would ever be legally required to have for the rest of my natural life, and I didn't know the first thing about anything in real life. I mean, what had they ever taught me about buying a car or a house or renting an apartment or buying a TV? Weren't you supposed to have insurance with those things? What about life insurance and hospital insurance? Or money? Where do you get the money to buy that stuff? Didn't my parents fight about money all the time? What the heck's life insurance anyway?

I thought about Sabrina Chavez. Beautiful, sweet, gorgeous, sable-haired Sabrina. What if she and I got married someday? How do you hold a wedding? Who buys the sandwiches and the ring and all that other crap? What're you supposed to say to get a girl to marry you anyway? And what about kids? I don't know anything about kids. I don't even *like* kids! Heck, I'm still a kid myself!

The hypotheticals poured down on me, a veritable flash flood of questions I had no idea how to answer. What about a job? How do you get a job? What would I do anyway? Play baseball? Be a rock star? Yeah, but what if they don't work out? Then what? Go work in a factory, or in a dull little office like the old man? Heck, no. Yeah, but then, how do you get into college? I know! The S.A.T. You take the S.A.T. Yeah, but there's gotta be more to it than that. There's an application or something, I think. And college is expensive. Wait! Nope, got that covered. The parental units will pay for college.

I don't get it. How come they don't teach you any of the stuff you need to know to get by in life? I don't even know how to get a checking account or a credit card. If they put me out on the street now, I'm screwed.

I scribbled and scratched notes about all the things I didn't know how to do, and by the time I had exhausted the list, it was twice as long as my graduation plan for high school. Worse, not one thing I needed to know- *nothing* -was even on the course list! So what was school for anyway? I wondered.

Learning how to know when you don't know all the answers, maybe?

LESSON 15

Tying One On

Mr. Dombrowski, the principal at Mountain View Junior High School, and I never agreed on anything. We were yin and yang; we were each other's special projects. I don't know what mysterious forces compel a principal to fashion a voodoo doll of one particular kid in school- maybe the kid puts the curse on himself -but in junior high school I was that kid. I told a joke at lunch one time that made Lucy Kidrow laugh so hard grape juice came spurting out of her nose and stained the front of her new dress. The next thing I knew, Mr. Dombrowski had me in his office.

"What'd I do?" I asked.

"You ruined Lucy Kidrow's dress," he said. "Her mother called me, and she's furious, I can tell you."

"All I did was tell a joke."

"Doesn't matter. You ruined her brand new dress. She's in tears."

"Tears of laughter maybe," I said. "It was a great joke, and she cracked up."

Mr. Dombrowski rapped his pencil on the top of his desk. "I don't like your attitude, Mr. Johnson."

"Me either, but what are you gonna do?"

"Mark my words, young man. That tone is not going to play well in your future. Here at Mountain View, or anywhere else."

That was how my conversations with Mr. Dombrowski typically went. No question, I was a marked man, Public Enemy

#1 at Mountain View Junior High School. In the teachers' eyes I was a clear and ever-present danger to the other students. Of course, most of my crimes were like the Lucy Kidrow grape juice incident: stupid things, like giving Jarod Schwartz a wedgie in the boys' locker room, or embarrassing our pre-algebra teacher Mrs. Picoult by imitating her in the hall outside her classroom. She was an easy mark for a smart aleck eighth grader because she pronounced her "r"s and "l"s like Elmer Fudd: "Okay, childwin, in this pwobwem you need to wocate the value of the missing vaweeable. So just weewax and concentwate. Hey, Mrs. Picoult, it's duck season! No, it's *wabbit* season!"

My most egregious offense, though, was that I refused to say the Pledge of Allegiance in the morning. Mr. Dombrowski *hated* that. He said I was unpatriotic and disrespectful for not reciting the pledge. I explained that it was my right as an American citizen to refuse to follow the herd. "Besides, it was written in 1892 by a Baptist preacher named Francis Bellamy," I said. "I'll bet you didn't know that."

"Of course I knew that," he said. "That doesn't excuse you from saying the pledge."

"Oh, you knew that, did you, Mr. Dombrowski? Why is it adults can never admit they're wrong or don't know something?"

"Because adults know more than kids do, that's why. Now-"

"Was 'under God' in the original pledge?"

"Yes, of course it was. Now-"

"Wrong. Congress added it in 1954 because they were scared of the Communists."

"Exactly! It's Communist, that's what it is!" he said. "Communist, pure and simple. My God, son, what kind of upbringing are your parents giving you?"

Mr. Dombrowski was the son of German immigrants and was a staunch believer in conformity and tradition. If you didn't conform and follow tradition you were an enemy of decency and all that was right with America. So it shouldn't have come as any surprise that when the last week of eighth grade rolled around, Mr. Dombrowski and I would cross swords one last time, just for old time's sake.

Now, Mountain View had a couple of going away traditions for the eighth graders each spring, sort of a bop on the butt for a job well done. They were Mr. Dombrowski's way of saying, "I'm proud you, kid; now g'won, get outta here, ya big palooka." Tradition number one was the three-day class trip to Washington, D.C. Tradition number two was a graduation ceremony on the last Monday night of the school year, complete with banners and bunting, speeches, flower arrangements, parents, grandparents, uncles- the works. The only things missing were the gowns and mortar board hats. The kids all thought it was corny, and you had to dress up nicely so your mom could take pictures and cry, but hey, if it got you out of the baby crib and into high school, it was worth it.

The one dress requirement that Mr. Dombrowski insisted all the boys wear was a necktie. I don't know a single boy who didn't groan when he heard that, except maybe Christopher Riglioni, but he was kind of an oddball and liked ties anyway. The only tie I owned was a silly little clip-on my mother had bought me for my great grandmother's funeral when I was ten, and even if I had known where to find it, it would have been too small for me. As it happened, I had been on a Jim Morrison/Moody Blues fashion jag in recent months and had saved up my allowance to buy a psychedelically vogue olive green paisley Apache tie. An

Apache tie was really just a scarf with a decorative clasp or ring, kind of like the scarf the Boy Scouts wore with their uniform, only it was infinitely hipper. But Dombrowski would never have allowed an Apache tie in his graduation ceremony, not in a thousand years.

"You can wear one of my ties," the old man suggested proudly.

"I don't want to wear a tie at all," I protested.

"Yes, I know, but since you have to, wear one of mine," he said.

"I don't even know how to tie a tie," I argued.

"No sweat. I'll tie it for you," he said.

Rats! He was cutting me off at every pass! I was trapped. I detested the idea of wearing a tie, and doubly hated it because it was Dombrowski's idea. He was a walking, talking, cranky thrill kill who had never had an original, creative thought in his life. His only reason for living was to piss on every kid's happiness. The more I thought about his edict, the angrier I got. Who was Dombrowski to tell me I had to wear a tie?

"The principal," my mother said.

"But what's the big deal about wearing a tie?" I whined. "It was originally a napkin for sloppy eaters. It had nothing to do with fashion."

"That may be," she said, "but it's fashion now, and all gentlemen wear a tie to formal occasions."

"Mom, the fashion now is the Apache tie, not the kind of tie Dad wears. I'll wear an Apache, but not a straight tie."

Mom stopped ironing my pants cuffs and thought for a moment. "Why don't you wear your Apache tie, then?" she said.

"There's no way Dombrowski would ever go for that," I said. "He wants it to be a regular necktie."

"Did he say specifically that it had to be a four-in-hand?" Mom asked.

"A four-in-what?"

"A four-in-hand. You know, a necktie like your father wears to work."

I thought back to the class assembly on Friday and tried to remember if Heir Dombrowski had ever said *specifically* what kind of tie the boys had to wear. Nope, all he said was "necktie." And what exactly is a necktie? A tie you wear around your neck. No specific style implied or stated. Ah-ha! I had him on a technicality!

"You're right," I told Mom. "He never said what kind of tie it had to be, he just said guys had to wear a tie. I'll wear my Apache."

The following Monday night was the big event. I wore my best pair of Navy blue slacks, dress socks and shoes, my freshly pressed and only white button down dress shirt, and my shiny, colorful, *hip* Apache necktie. My parents and kid brother all dressed up too, as if we were going to a baptism, and we piled into the Fairlane, headed for the first graduation in the family since my promotion from kindergarten to the first grade.

Just as a precaution, the old man had taken down one of his neckties and had my mother stuff it into her pocketbook, despite my objections. "Humor me," he said.

Fine. I'll humor you. Whatever that *means.*

My mother was obsessed with time, and we arrived early enough for the three of them to grab front row seats in the auditorium while I made my way backstage. A couple of dozen boys were already in the choir room, tucking in their shirts, combing their hair, and . . . fixing their ties. Their regular, ordinary neckties. I was the only boy there with a different kind of tie on. Groovy, I thought. I was different than everybody else. Exactly what I wanted. Take *that*, Dombrowski. You might be able to lord tall over all of these other sheep, but not me, brother. Not me!

Just then I felt a tap on my shoulder. I turned around and looked directly into the gold plated clasp of Mr. Dombrowski's maroon and white striped tie, straight as a ruler down the front of his shirt. "Mr. Johnson," he said, "what is that around your neck?"

I fingered the wide gold ring holding fast to my Apache tie and with a hint of arrogance said, "My tie."

Dombrowski's already stern expression turned unsettlingly dour. "That, sir, is not a tie. I suggest you find another, more suitable form of necktie if you'd like to participate in tonight's graduation ceremony. You have fifteen minutes."

"What's wrong with this one?" I asked.

"It's not an acceptable tie for this occasion, Mr. Johnson, as you very well know."

"But what's an 'acceptable tie for this occasion'? You never said what kind of tie we had to have. You just said we had to have a tie. I have a tie."

"Mr. Johnson, I have no intention of standing here debating with you. Now go change your tie, or go home."

The backstage area was rapidly filling up with throngs of eighth graders, many of them my friends, and every one of them with a standard necktie on. Had I missed something? What happened to taking a stand? What happened to individuality and protest? This was the 60s. *Do the names Mick Jagger and Abby Hoffman mean anything to you people?*

Panicked, I made my way into the auditorium, which was rapidly filling with parents and other family members, and walked over to my parents. "Dombrowski's done it to me again," I growled.

"What's he done?" asked my dad.

"He wants me to wear a regular tie. He won't let me wear my Apache."

The old man smiled derisively. "Told you."

"Gee, thanks, Dad."

Mom reached into her pocketbook and pulled out the emergency tie she had brought for just this circumstance. "Here," she said. "Put this on instead."

I started to yank off my Apache tie when a moment of clarity came over me. I glanced at the hundreds of fathers and brothers in the audience and saw that every one of them, without apparent exception, was wearing a tie: a traditional four-in-hand necktie. So was every boy backstage. Something was terribly wrong here, but I wasn't sure what it was. All I knew was that I was at odds with the entire assembly. I didn't belong there.

"No, I don't think so," I said.

"Don't be silly," Mom said. "Let Dad tie it for you, and you can go though graduation."

"Mom, I can't. He never said what kind of tie we had to wear, and now he's trying to set the rules at the last minute. It's not fair."

"It's no big deal," the old man said. I could tell by his tone that he was getting frustrated with me. "We all got dressed up to come here and watch you graduate the eighth grade. I for one would very much like to see you cooperate for once."

"But it's not fair!" By this time I had the attention of several other parents as well as my own. "He's changing the rules at the last minute!"

"Heath, don't be so stubborn," my mother pleaded.

"I can't do it, Mom. It's just wrong all over the place."

"Fine," the old man said in a huff. "Let's go."

With that, he took my mother by the hand and stood, who in turn took David by the hand and stood, who in turn looked at me as if I had just done the dumbest thing in the world, and in a very unhappy procession- me trailing the rest of my family -we walked out of the Mountain View Junior High School auditorium.

To this day, I have never returned to Mountain View. On several visits back to Somerville over the forty-something years since, I have never even been able to find it. But in my mind, something great and grand took place there once. On a Monday night in 1968.

LESSON 16
First Love

"Master: Boatswain!

Boatswain: Here, Master! What cheer!

Master: Good. Speak to th' mariners. Fall to't, yarely, or we run ourselves aground- bestir, bestir!"

Mrs. Fitch looked up from her massive, intimidatingly thick volume of *The Complete Works of Shakespeare,* and with sinister eyes scanned the class, a captive gathering of 14-year-old freshmen English students so befuddled by the words she had just read, that she might as well have been a Pentecostal Sunday school teacher speaking in tongues.

What the heck's a "boatswain?" I wondered. *"Yarely"? Is that the same as "yearly?"*

Sabrina Chavez, the ever-studious and raven-haired beauty who sat beside me in the next row, stuck a pencil in the center of her paperback "Tempest" as if she were already surrendering and cast a worried look at me.

I cupped my hand in front of my mouth and tried to get her attention. "Pssst! Sabrina!" I whispered, almost inaudibly, "What's a boatswain?" I figured if anybody in class had a clue what a boatswain was, it would be Sabrina.

I have no idea, she mouthed back.

Oh-oh. If luscious, academically perfect Sabrina didn't know what Mrs. Fitch and Shakespeare were talking about, what chance did I have?

"And so, ladies and gentlemen, sweet scholars, and all the rest of you," continued Mrs. Fitch, "we begin one of William Shakespeare's most enduring tragedies, *The Tempest*. It is a tale about the inhabitants of a small island in the sea, which had been enchanted by a witch named Sycorax, who had died a short time before the inhabitants of the island, an old man, whose name was Prospero, and who had been deposited onto the island by mysterious chance, and his daughter Miranda, who was very beautiful. Now, the two of them lived together in a cave, and because Prospero was a student of magic and kept all of his books on the subject in his part of the cave, and because he found magic to be very useful, he had been able to release many good spirits that Sycorax had imprisoned in the bodies of trees because they had refused to carry out her evil orders. And because Prospero had done these benevolent spirits a good turn by releasing them, the main spirit being Ariel, they promised their undying obedience and loyalty to Prospero."

John Pickle raised his hand.

"Yes, John?"

"I have no idea what you're talking about."

"Me either," added Deanie Savagei.

"Yeah, what's any of that got to do with a boatswain?" chimed Sammy Napolitano.

"Nothing," said Mrs. Fitch.

The whole class jumped in at once then, everyone complaining louder than everyone else. "It's too hard to understand." "They don't speak English." "Why do we have to learn this?" All the usual objections to reading Shakespeare.

Mrs. Fitch stood stone-faced and waited for us to get it all out of our systems. Finally, when the last of us caught on that she was waiting for us to knock it off, she flipped the pages of her Shakespeare tome and asked, "Has it ever occurred to any of you budding literati, that there is a very sound and worthwhile reason why William Shakespeare is still taught and performed the world over, even after four centuries have passed since he drew his last breath?"

Sabrina raised her hand. "Because he's good?"

Mrs. Fitch rolled her eyes. "Well, yes, dear, of course he's good. But what *makes* him good? What makes him relevant to us today?"

Several others took a stab at the answer, but no one came up with the response Mrs. Fitch was looking for. "Well, she said at last, "since no one seems to know the value of Mr. Shakespeare's work, here's what I propose. I propose that we table our Shakespearean studies for the time being and concentrate instead on the opening movement to our poetry unit, beginning with the sonnet."

Groans rippled throughout the room. "Ugh. Poetry."

"Well, it's either that or Shakespeare. We have to cover both units this term. It doesn't matter what order." The class voted to go with the poetry and put off Shakespeare as long as possible, but as fas as I was concerned it was like choosing between Brussels sprouts and beets. "And I'll tell you what," she added. "I think maybe *The Tempest* may be a little bit above your pay grade right now, so when we do study Master Shakespeare, we'll read *Romeo and Juliet* instead, okay?"

More groans.

"Now, now, now. What possible objections can you have to *Romeo and Juliet*?"

"Lame-o," protested Deanie Savage.

"In what sense, Deanie?"

"It's not realistic. It's romantic crap."

"Well, thank you for that deep and insightful review, Miss Savage. I take it you've read *Romeo and Juliet*?"

"No, not exactly."

"I see. How many of you have read the play?" No one raised his hand. "How many of you are familiar with the basic story?" Almost every hand went up. "Okay, can anyone tell me how old Romeo and Juliet were?"

Several hands went up, including Sabrina's.

I should mention at this point that my crush on Sabrina Chavez, which was now several years old, was stronger than ever. Not only was she as pretty as a Spanish garden, she was also the smartest girl in the ninth grade and smelled heavenly. I had known her since the fifth grade and worshipped her from afar. I dreamed about her at night and wrote her name with mine inside my notebook on every page, but I had never had the courage to tell her how I felt about her. I was in love with the idea of being in love with her, but she didn't know.

"Sabrina, what do you think?"

"About seventeen or eighteen?"

"No. Anybody else? Larry?"

"I'm guessing they were in their early twenties. I mean, they were old enough to marry, right?"

"Yes, they were, but actually, Larry, they were probably right around your age. They were probably about fourteen."

Several girls squealed. "Fourteen? Ewww! That's too young."

"Too young to be in love?" Mrs. Fitch surveyed the class. "Let's think about something. Most of you are starting to notice a difference in each other, am I right? I don't just mean physical differences-" giggles and hoots erupted from everyone in the room "-yes, yes, let it all out, you erudite paramours. No, what I mean is that besides the obvious anatomical changes you see in each other, you're also beginning to appreciate each other in new ways. You girls see boys in a new emotional light, and, it is to be hoped, you boys see the young ladies in a new emotional light as well." There were more snickers and grunts of suppressed laughter, but not as many this time.

"Anyway, the point is, if it hasn't already happened to you, it's going to very soon. You girls: you see that special someone, maybe somebody you've known since kindergarten, and all of a sudden, one day, he looks completely different to you. It's not how tall he is, or his developing muscles, or that his voice seems to have dropped a little lower in his throat. The fact is, you don't know what it is that's different, but there's something about him that makes it seem as if he is a whole new person you're seeing for the very first time.

"You young men: one day you're teasing the girl who sits beside you in math because she's just a girl you've always known and she's never taken you seriously, and the next day you're doing a dance with the moon and the stars, writing her name in your notebook, singing every love song you hear on the radio to her. Oh, it's ridiculous, how we get when we're in love."

Life Lessons 101

I could tell some of the other kids, not just me, were getting a little unnerved by what Mrs. Fitch was saying, even though most of them were trying to hide it.

Christopher Riglioni, ever the intellectual adventurer, raised his hand. I always thought he was kind of slow, but sometimes I wondered if he wasn't putting us on, that he was really serving as point man for all the kids in the class who were too chicken to ask the questions for themselves.

"Yes, Christopher?"

"What's this got to with Shakespeare?"

"Ah! I'm glad you asked. What your impending romances have to do with Shakespeare is that Mr. Shakespeare understood human nature- and young people in particular -better than just about anyone else. He knew that the most overpowering, debilitating, mesmerizing, *passionate* love that ever strikes a human being is the first love. It's the love that has you sitting up at your bedroom window in the middle of the night staring at the full moon and dreaming about the one you adore, the love who takes away your appetite and makes you a blithering idiot twenty-four hours a day. You'll do absolutely anything for her, and you'll swear you'll be together forever. You'd rather be dead than live without her. It's called First Love.

"So if you're William Shakespeare and you want to write a play about two lovers doing a dance with the moon and the stars, what better scenario than a pair of fourteen-year-olds in absolutely hopeless love for the first time and whose parents forbid them to see each other? What love could be more powerful than one that makes you willing to die for each other when you haven't even started to live? Believe me, that's the stuff of prime time TV. Why do we study Shakespeare, and 'Romeo and Juliet' in particular?

No emotional experience you ever live through in your life will be more intense than the one you're about to have. Except the death of someone near and dear to you, perhaps, but that's for another time."

"I suppose Shakespeare has a play for that too?" John blurted, to a few uneasy chortles.

"Indeed, indeed," said Mrs. Fitch. "Well, enough of that. On to the poetry. If you will, please, put away your Shakespeare and take out your textbooks. Turn to page 322, 'The Highwayman.'"

I don't know if anybody else in the class gave another thought to what Mrs. Fitch had said about First Love, but I did. For the whole rest of the period I couldn't take my eyes off Sabrina. Everything about her made me tingle. The way she would tuck her black shoulder-length hair behind her ear, the way her lips moved when she spoke silently to herself, the rise and fall of her chest as she breathed. But more- much more -I began to wonder what she thought about when there was no one around. I wondered what made her happiest and what frightened her. I thought of walking through the woods with her across a pristine blanket of freshly fallen snow. In my mind, I became one with her.

I had never believed it was possible that I could have so many questions about a girl, yet I wanted to know everything about her. I knew someday she would break my heart and I would never fully recover, but I didn't care. All that mattered was the girl sitting beside me in the next row. The way the flu sneaks up on you- a sniffle, a vague aching all over, the first warming of an oncoming fever -I felt the gentle, initial pangs of First Love overtaking me. It wouldn't be long before I had the courage to tell Sabrina how I felt about her.

But until then, I would go home and wait for the moon to rise. Then, I would read *Romeo and Juliet* and learn more about this thing called First Love.

LESSON 17

Veterans' Day

If you were a long-haired 15-year-old boy in 1970 and you got more from a Jefferson Airplane album than you ever got out of school or those deep and meaningful "man talks" with your father, you dreamed of living somewhere far away from home. You idolized Bob Dylan and Jim Morrison and Jimi Hendrix. You hung on every note they played, every word they sang; you wanted to be like them, sound like them, look like them. Long hair was a way to express your contempt for the establishment; to say to the adults and conformists all around you, *I reject the rules you live by. I think for myself. I represent my generation.*

In my mind this was a heroic stand to take. Part of my one-man protest against social compliance was my refusal to say the Pledge of Allegiance in school. This puzzled some of my classmates, amused others, and universally annoyed my teachers. But you have to remember: this was at a time when my family, like millions of other American families, sat down to dinner each night with war on TV. In Vietnam the body count was rising on both sides, and every evening we were compelled to watch news footage of dead and wounded American soldiers being dragged through rice paddies under enemy fire to hovering helicopters, and all the while thinking about the neighbors down the street whose own sons were in Vietnam at that very moment. Even at the predictably naive age of fifteen I had already figured out that something in what the government was telling us about Vietnam wasn't adding up.

For my fifteenth birthday my parents bought me a new blue Schwinn ten speed bicycle, and for the rest of May and every day that summer I rode that bike everywhere. Into town, to the bowling alley, down to the river, to Martins' Market, to friends' houses, everywhere. Once I rode it all the way to Morristown, almost thirty miles away.

So it happened that on a particularly sultry July afternoon I had ridden my bike down little two lane Highway 28, down to what was affectionately and familiarly known as The Somerville Circle (an insane free-for-all traffic configuration that had obviously been designed by a bunch of drunk architects) that swirled local traffic around its concrete center either toward downtown, out to Highway 22, or into the waiting brick and glass store fronts of the A & P shopping center. The shopping center was home to the single most important destination of my entire youth: the R & B Record Store. Not a weekend went by that I wasn't sorting through the R & B record bins looking for the latest albums by my favorite groups. Occasionally I was able to buy an album if I had saved up my allowance, but this time I hadn't bought anything, being a couple of dollars short of the cash I needed to pick up the Doors' third album. I was riding lazily along the shoulder of the road on my way back home when a dull grey pickup truck slowed down beside me and someone inside flung the remains of his sloppy sandwich and a cup of chili on me.

"Get a haircut, faggot!" the truck's passenger shouted. Then all three riders howled with laughter and yelled obscenities as the driver gunned the engine and sped away.

"Real brave, you bunch of inbreds!" I yelled back. I was furious and not thinking, so I added a little hand gesture for emphasis to let them know I didn't like wearing their lunch remains. Unfortunately, the instant I thrust my finger in the air I wished I hadn't, and I hoped they hadn't seen me. After all, there were three of them. I'd get killed.

But they *did* see me. Suddenly, the bright red brake lights of the truck flashed on, and I knew I was in trouble. The driver threw the truck in reverse and huge plumes of grey smoke erupted from under the rear tires as he spun his wheels to gain traction. Panicked, I searched for a way to escape. The easiest thing to do was to duck into the woods beside the road, but there was no way I could ride my bike through the underbrush- not fast enough to get away from three guys on foot, anyway -and I didn't intend to leave my brand new bike behind for them to steal or destroy. I thought of turning around and riding the other way as fast as I could, but they were in a truck; no way I could outrun them. Terrified, I froze and watched them screeching backward toward me, recklessly backing up toward the one car down the road behind them. It was a little blue Rambler, and I thought, *Yeh! Thank God for Mr. Businessman. They won't do anything now.*

But I was wrong. Mr. Businessman slammed on his brakes to avoid rear-ending the pickup and then swerved into the oncoming lane to go around, since there was no traffic coming the other way.

"Crazy stupid teenagers!" he hollered. "You trying to get us all killed?" With what little engine power he had, Mr. Businessman floored his accelerator, and with a concentrated puff of exhaust from the tailpipe, he and his Rambler were off down the road. Meanwhile, the driver of the pickup had maneuvered onto the shoulder of the road ahead of me, effectively cutting me off. Both doors swung open, and out poured three rednecks, complete with camouflage hunting vests, John Deere hats, flush red cheeks, oversized buckles, and holstered pocketknives.

"You got a real attitude problem, you know that, queer bait?" said the one on the passenger side as all three walked toward me. It was a dangerous moment, but I couldn't help noticing he was slightly cross-eyed. Funny how you notice little details like that when your life is in danger.

"You a hippie?" the driver said, spitting a big gob of brown liquid at the blacktop.

"He's a hippie, all right," assessed the guy in the middle.

I didn't say anything. What *could* I say? Still straddling my bike, all I could think of was how sad it was going to make my mother later when she came to visit me in the intensive care unit and how my old man would explode when he saw my brand new bike destroyed. To him, it would be like losing a member of the family.

"I can't stand hippie queers," said the passenger, tipping his hat brim up a touch.

"You need a haircut, ya pansy," said the middle guy, fingering the snap of the knife case on his belt.

"You don't have to do this," I said, quivering. "I'm sorry, really. I didn't mean it. Honest. Just leave me alone, and you'll never see me again."

The driver and passenger moved to either side of me; I could smell the tobacco and onion on their breath. "Hold him, down, while I give him a trim," said the one in the middle. He pulled out his knife, and I felt my knees go weak as they dragged me off my bike and pressed me down on the shady side of the ground beside the truck. All I remember feeling is points of gravel digging into the back of my head and the full weight of a knee on my chest. I fought and kicked, but they were too strong. The last thing I recall seeing was a glint of sunlight off the tip of the knife blade, and then . . .

The sound of an engine and tires sliding in the gravel, followed by a vehicle door opening and slamming. And shouting. *Lots* of shouting. One by one the three attackers were yanked off me. I heard thuds, as if sacks of concrete were being tossed into the bed of the pickup. Suddenly I was alone on the ground, my hands and arms free, nothing but daylight above me. Cautiously, I lifted my head and saw a man in green military fatigues pinning the guy with the knife up against the tailgate of the truck with the palm of one hand pressed up under the assailant's chin, the other wedged against his throat. " . . . anyone else, either, you hear me?" I heard him growl. "That goes for all three of you! I see you anywhere near this boy again, they'll need cadaver dogs to find all the pieces. You're dealing with the United States Army now, son! You comprende?"

The passenger was rubbing his neck, the driver holding his ribs and trying to catch his breath. The one with the knife had his hands on the man's arm but couldn't budge it. "I asked you a question, boy!" the man repeated.

"You're choking me," he said through clenched teeth.

The man adjusted his grip on the knife-wielder's throat to stress the urgency of his question. "What'd you say to me?"

"You're choking me," the guy repeated, garbling his words.

"Yes, I am," said the man. "Now, for the third and final time, do you unnerstand that if you ever come near this young man again it *will* cost you your life?"

Life Lessons 101

"Yes!"

"Yes, *what*?"

"Yes, sir!"

The man released his hold and stepped back. "Good. Now, you and your girlfriends here have got five seconds to get gone before I lose my temper. Five seconds. One one thousand . . . two one thousand . . ."

The three derelicts scrambled to the cab of the truck and before my rescuer could say *five one thousand*, they were speeding away, shouting obscenities and giving us both the finger.

By now I was standing up and brushing myself off, stunned and dazed by what had just happened. I was immensely grateful to this stranger, whoever he was, but all I wanted to do was get home. There was something about him that told me I had simply traded one kind of trouble for another. I was distrustful of adults anyway, having had run-ins with them at home and at school for the better part of three years now, so the only thing on my mind was getting on my bike and riding away as fast as I could.

"You all right?" the man asked as he walked over to me.

"Yes, fine," I said, still a little shaky from the ordeal. "Wow. Thanks."

"My pleasure," he said, and he held out his hand. "R.K. Lang, Lieutenant, United States Army."

"Yes, sir," I said, shaking his hand. "I'm Heath."

"Glad to meet you, Heath. So tell me, what'd you say to get those boys so worked up?"

"I didn't say anything. I was just riding my bike and they threw food at me and yelled a bunch of insults."

"Decided to give you a haircut, too, it looks like."

"I don't know what they were going to do. I'm just glad you came along and they didn't get a chance to do it."

"Well, you got that long hair, I guess you've gotta be used to people telling you you look like a girl and calling you a queer."

"Used to it? No. I hear it all the time, but I never get used to it."

"Maybe you *should* get a haircut, then."

"Yeah, maybe I should. But I don't think I will."

"It doesn't matter. I don't think those boys were going to hurt you. They were just out having some fun, you know? Blowing off a little steam. Over in 'Nam some of the boys in my company'll shoot at the villagers for fun. They got no intention of hurting them, really; they're just trying to get rid of the jumps. Anyway-"

I picked up my bicycle and set it up on the kickstand. "You've been in Vietnam?" I asked. Even though four guys in my neighborhood had gone to Vietnam and it was on the news every night, I had never actually seen nor met a combat soldier who had been there. I was intrigued.

"Just got back," he said. "R and R for two weeks, then I go back. I've re-upped three times, but I'm calling it quits after this next one. I've got other things to do besides kill dinks."

I was flabbergasted. "You've actually killed people?"

"Some VC, yeah. What about you? You don't look ready yet, but you *are* going to help your country when the time comes, right?"

"I'm not sure what you mean," I said.

"You're what, fifteen, sixteen?"

"Fifteen," I said.

"Come on, walk and talk," he said, gesturing for me to join him as he turned to walk to his truck. For the first time I noticed his ride, a dark green Ford pickup with a white camper top on the back. "Sure," I said, and I followed him to the back of his truck.

"What I mean is, we've got lots of guys over there who gripe and moan about how they didn't ask to be there, don't want to be there, blah, blah, blah. A real bunch of crybabies. Not the officers, of course, but those infantry wussies, my god! You look like a kid who knows something about patriotism, not like some of those ingrates I have to deal with. Can't say I care for all that hair, but you join up and the Army'll lop it all off and make a man out of you."

"I don't know," I said. "No disrespect intended, but I don't like the Army. I'm against the war."

"Is that right?" he said, opening the back door of his camper and climbing inside. I could tell he had been on the road for a long time, or at least it looked like it, because he had a makeshift bed made up of a small mattress and pillow crammed against the left side, a portable stove with crusty pots and pans on it on top of a military issue footlocker, piles of dirty clothes, green ammunition boxes, and trash. "Well, tell me, Heath old buddy, what exactly do you know about the war?"

I had to think about my answer because I was sure that no matter what I said he wasn't going to like it. He was a grown-up, and nothing I stood for or said ever pleased a grown-up. The best I could do was choose my words carefully and try not to make him angry. "Well," I began, "I know that three guys in my neighborhood were drafted and got killed."

"Mm-hmm." He started moving things around in the camper in an attempt to straighten it up a bit. "What else?"

"I know we're not supposed to be there. It's not even a declared war."

He chuckled at that. "Not a war, I like that. What else?"

"Um . . . we're losing, and most Americans don't support it."

He *didn't* like that. He stopped shuffling things around and stared straight at me, his eyes dark and fierce. "What the hell do they know about winning and losing? People don't support us because they don't have any idea what's going on or why it's happening." Then, his expression brightened and he returned to the business of rearranging his living quarters.

"See, the thing civilians at home don't unnerstand is that the dinks are trying to take over the whole continent. If we let them get a toehold over there, next thing you know Nebraskans are wearing pointy straw hats, eating with chopsticks, and carrying pictures of Chairman Mao."

"Wow," I mused. "That's just what John Lennon said."

"What's that?"

"He said, 'But if you go carrying pictures of Chairman Mao, you ain't gonna make it with anyone anyhow.'"

"Hmm. Well, anyway, the thing about this war is that it isn't like World War II where everyone knew who the enemy was and you could spot him easy. In 'Nam you never know who the enemy is and who your friends are. They all look the same. Same silly hats, same slant eyes, same pajamas. North, South- a dink's a dink. You're in the middle of the jungle in some pot sticker village, and there's this girl, maybe she's eighteen, twenty years old; she's sweet and friendly as she can be, maybe she's pregnant, and she's telling your company's interrogator that her husband was killed by the VC and that she's on your side. All those woven vats of rice are for the village not the Vietcong regulars, and against your better judgment, you believe her. You blow up the rice anyway because you don't want it to fall into enemy hands, and you burn the huts and dynamite the bunkers below them because you can't take the chance that the bunkers aren't hideouts for VC, and you leave, knowing that you just destroyed her home, her food, and everything she's got in this world. You feel awful, but it's your job. *That's* what you see and hear on the news. American soldiers: baby killers, monsters running rampant across the Vietnamese countryside burning everything in sight."

I have to admit, I was transfixed. It was one thing to hear and read about these things in Life magazine, or see it on the C.B.S. Evening News, but it was a whole other experience to be standing there listening to a man who had seen these things with his own eyes. Even more compelling, he had actually done them.

"See, that's just what I'm talking about," I said.

His preparations in the back of the camper, whatever they were for, were almost complete. With military efficiency he had transformed a veritable pig stye into a smartly arranged sleeping and living compartment. It made me wonder how and why he had allowed his camper to get into such disarray.

"Yeah, well. What they don't tell you on the news is that right after you leave feeling awful because you scared the hell out of that girl and torched her village, she watches your company walk down the trail and get blown up by a booby trap that she knew was there, but didn't tell you about. Turns out she's VC, or a VC sympathizer, and might have even placed it there herself. Charlie's everywhere, son. You can't trust anybody. That's what *I'm* talking about."

I hated to admit it, but he had a point. What was a soldier in Vietnam supposed to do when he didn't know who the enemy was, who he could trust, and worst, knew that the majority of the people back home didn't trust *him*?

"Do you live around here?" I asked. I remembered what he had said to my attackers about leaving their parts scattered around the state if they ever bothered me again. How would he know they had come near me again unless he lived in the area and we happened to run into each other again?

"Nope," he said. "I'm drifting, on my way up to Maine."

That was odd. Why would he be on insignificant little Highway 28 when Somerville was an exit off the Garden State Parkway which bisected New Jersey and took you straight through to New York?

He had finished his housecleaning now and was sitting on the tailgate of his truck, looking for all the world like a man relaxed and at peace with himself. "This is a pretty area," he said. "You must live nearby."

"Through these woods," I told him, pointing off to my right. "I really should be getting home. My mom's going to be wondering where I am. I left the house three hours ago."

"What about your dad? Was he ever in the military?"

"He was in the Navy in World War II, but he never saw any action. He had a desk job, from what I understand. Hey, listen, I've really got to get going."

"Oh sure, sure." He hopped off the tailgate and gave me a wide, ingratiating smile. "Hey, listen, before you go, I wonder if you could give me a hand with something."

I couldn't imagine what he might need help with. He was a pretty stout soldier who had seen action in Vietnam, and he had managed to straighten out his entire camper lodgings in the span of a five-minute conversation. How could he need me? Still, he had come to my rescue, and in truth, I suddenly had a new respect for the Army, or, at least, *this* soldier. "Sure," I said. "What do you need?"

"I forgot that right rear tire is going flat and I just realized that the crank to pull my spare tire from out underneath the truck and loosen the lug nuts is in the back of the camper underneath all that stuff I just finished moving around and stacking. Can you help me get to it? If we work together I can get at it and get the tire changed in half the time."

To be honest, I didn't feel like helping him do what amounted to a garage cleaning- I was nervous now and trying to think of an excuse to get home -but, as I say, I felt I owed him the favor. "Yeah, okay," I said. "What do you need me to do?"

"If you'll climb in and start handing me things, I'll stack them out here out of the way, and we can get to the crank faster and easier than if I had to dig and feel my way around. I think I know where it is, but I'm not sure. You're young and strong; you can move around back there easier than I can."

I was hesitant, again, because I didn't want to do manual labor in the middle of a hot summer day, in the back of some stranger's truck. But, I owed him . . .

"Yeah, oaky," I said, and I hopped up into the bed of the camper. "Where do you want me to start?" I asked. When I didn't get an immediate answer, I looked over my shoulder and saw U.S. Army Lieutenant R. K. Lang climbing in after me, effectively blocking my view out the back.

"How about with a kiss?" he said.

A dizzying, sweeping chill overcame me. I felt I was going to be sick, and retreated as far back into the corner of the camper as I possibly could, coiled and terrified. "Get away from me!" I shrieked.

"Settle down, son, settle down," he said. "I'm not going to hurt you. You're too sweet to hurt."

"Jesus!" I shouted. "Get away!"

"Now, now, is that any way to treat a Vietnam veteran? I just want a little love, that's all. A little appreciation for my service to my country."

"God, you're sick!" I said, every part of my body trembling. "Leave me alone!"

"Now, now. Just play along, and it will all be over before you know it. Who knows? You might even like it. I didn't think I'd like it either, the first time." He crawled toward me and made a playful come-to-me expression. "Now, why don't you just relax and-"

Before he could get the next syllable out I chambered my leg and kicked him in the face with all my might. The heel of my shoe hit him square in the mouth and his head snapped back in a burst of blood and broken teeth. He screamed and flopped over on his side, blood pouring through his hands, cupped over his mouth. He was writhing in pain, but was in no condition to grab me as I clamored out the back of the truck, jumped on my bicycle, and slung up the kickstand as I peeled out in a spray of gravel and dirt. As I pedaled maniacally to gather as much speed as possible, I could hear him screaming obscenities and vowing to kill me if he ever found out where I lived. I pedaled as fast and as hard as I could, and in a matter of minutes I was safely home, the garage door closed and locked, and every window and door in the house bolted shut.

"Heath, what's wrong?" my mother asked, clearly alarmed at my behavior and following me around the house as I checked each window and door a second time. "What in the world has gotten into you?"

I ran up to my room and closed the door without answering her, though she followed me upstairs and stood at my door knocking repeatedly. "Heath! Heath, let me in, sweetheart. Tell me what's wrong." But I couldn't let her in, and I couldn't tell her what had happened. I *never* told her what happened that hot summer afternoon in 1970, not to her dying day.

You see, her brother- my uncle John Clay -had been a lieutenant in the United States Army also, in World War II. First Battalion, 175th Infantry, 29th Division. Everyone in our family knew the story. He was serving in France as company commander, shortly after his captain had been killed by a booby trap when, on the morning of September 11, he and his men were ordered to attack and seize an area known as Keriel farms. My uncle and his runner went forward to make a quick preliminary reconnaissance of the area before deploying the rest of the company, and as my uncle peered over a hedge to get a better view, he was shot and killed by a sniper's bullet.

It was a story I had heard before, but because I never knew my uncle, its importance and value were lost on me in my youth. Only many years later did its significance become apparent to me. It came with the birth of my first son, whom my wife and I named after Lieutenant John Clay. From the very first day we found out we were going to have a son, one of the questions she and I pondered was, what do we do if the day ever comes when our son is asked- or worse, compelled -to go to war?

It is my hope that if wiser men are leading nations then, it may be a question we'll never have to answer, and neither will he. But in the meantime, I ask myself another question: if it was impossible to distinguish who was the enemy and who was the friend in Vietnam, how is it possible to discern among the soldiers I honor on Veteran's Day, who is the friend and who is the enemy?

LESSON 18

Love's As Durable as Rice Paper

Valerie and I were in love. I mean richly, passionately, *hopelessly* in love. Oblivious to everything and everyone else in the world love.

I was seventeen, she was sixteen. We had been having romantic, idyllic conversations about what it would be like to get married ever since our first kiss in the entranceway to the pump room below the community swimming pool. By the autumn of my junior year in high school, we were so ridiculously in love that all common sense and whatever reason we had possessed at the start of our relationship had gone so missing that the Coast Guard and NASA couldn't have found them. There were times when I thought I would suffocate if I didn't have her in my arms. Likewise, Valerie devoted every breath she took to me.

That Christmas my family traveled to Sarasota, Florida, to spend the holiday with my grandparents, and I thought I was going to die. It was bad enough to have to spend Christmas at the beach in sunny 85-degree weather, but to be dragged away from my love, my princess, was more than I could bear. She and I exchanged presents in my driveway the morning we left, hugged and kissed each other goodbye, and as my old man gunned our new Ford Torino, which he had nicknamed "the Blue Oiler" for some reason, I waved a sad, solemn goodbye to Valerie.

We had been a steady couple for almost a year and a half, and nothing and no one had come between us. Not even her former boyfriend Robby Vetere, who picked a fight with me in front of the whole school in the gym one afternoon after lunch- and lost -could wedge his way between us. We were wrapped around each other, inseparable and star-crossed.

But when the snows melted and the ground thawed in March, something totally unexpected happened. I walked Valerie to class one day, just as I always had, gave her a quick kiss outside Mrs. Henshaw's room, and then headed to class myself. But when I turned the corner down the science hall, I spotted Lisa McDooley coming the other way, flanked by a pair of her cheerleader cronies.

As head cheerleader, Lisa was strictly out of my league, but that never stopped me from fantasizing about her now and then. Heck, every guy I knew fantasized about Lisa McDooley. Even in the dead of winter she had the silkiest, shiniest hair; a perfect creamy mocha complexion; the sexy, alluring eyes of a goddess; and a blindingly white, perfect smile. Lisa McDooley had an aura about her of transcendent, delicate splendor. If you were a guy and Lisa McDooley deigned to even glance in your direction, you would be high and full of yourself for the rest of the day.

Oh, really? Chrissy Buffington spoke to you in the lunch line today? Am I supposed to be impressed? Lisa McDooley smiled at me today!

That was the trump card: a smile from Lisa McDooley. Of course, you knew you still had no chance with her whatsoever, but that wasn't the point. The point was that she had noticed you; she actually knew you existed. After a nod or smile from Lisa McDooley, all other miracles faded in comparison.

So there I was, walking toward my biology lab at the end of the hall, when I saw Lisa McDooley coming the other way. I figured I was going to get a good eyeful, enough to sustain me for the next fifty excruciating minutes with Mr. Burr and his frozen lab rats, and that alone was enough to put a spring in my step. I tried to look nonchalant, but I didn't want to miss my chance to get a good look at her, either. She was camping it up with the other girls- *my God, look at those delicious teeth! What I wouldn't give to kiss that mouth just one time!* -when all three of them turned coyly toward the boys behind them and giggled. Suddenly, Lisa's two friends peeled away and ducked into classrooms on either side of the hallway, just as the tardy bell rang. There were only a couple of wandering, defiant strays left in the hall now, all of us late to class, and Lisa was one of them. She was fifteen feet away, so it was impossible for us not to at least make eye contact, unless we deliberately looked away from each other, and why would we do that?

Ten feet.

Five feet.

All at once I was face-to-face with a beautiful wide Lisa McDooley smile and wink. "Hi, Heath!"

I uttered a shell-shocked but nonetheless casual-sounding "Hey," in response, and in an instant the whole magnificent encounter was over. So quickly did it end that I wondered if I had imagined it. High with the adrenaline rush of a personal greeting from Lisa McDooley herself, and wanting to be sure she had been intentionally speaking to me and not someone else, I shot a quick, desperate look back down the hall just in time to see her twist her neck to catch a last fleeting glance of me too.

I slipped into Mr. Burr's room unnoticed as he called roll and took my place at the lab counter in the back corner. Over and over I asked myself, *What just happened? Did Lisa McDooley just speak to me? Did she just say "hi" to me? Why? She doesn't even know me. Unless . . . Unless she went to the trouble to find out who I was. Oh, man. If she asked around and found out my name . . .*

My brain swam with images of Lisa and the possibilities for our future together. *Oh, my God! My life has just changed! Everything has just changed! Lisa McDooley and me! I can't believe it!*

"Mr. Johnson!"

With a look on my face that must have resembled post traumatic stress disorder, I looked up from my reverie to see Mr. Burr staring down over his half moon glasses at me.

"Huh?"

"Mr. Johnson, are you alive in there?"

Embarrassed and lightheaded at the same time, I smiled weakly. "I think so."

"Okay. Just checking. You look a little dazed."

I was giddy for the rest of the day, bursting with my secret, but not daring to let Valerie know what I knew. That she and I were done, and Lisa and I were about to light each other's lanterns.

Late the next afternoon, as the sun was setting and Valerie and I were walking hand-in-hand along the shore of Concord Lake, I jumped off the highest cliff of my life. When we reached our favorite trysting spot I gently withdrew my hand from hers and rammed it into my pocket. "We need to talk," I said.

Valerie was no Rhodes Scholar, but she was smart enough to know that nothing good ever follows the phrase, "We need to talk." Her happy expression immediately changed. Her eyes were concerned and shadowed. "About what?"

"I think we need to stop seeing each other," I said bluntly.

Her jaw dropped. "What?"

"Well, I've been thinking. We've been together almost two years now, and I just thought that maybe we ought to-"

"Two wonderful years, Heath! We've been together two wonderful, happy years! We're going to be married someday. We're going to be together for the rest of our lives. You're not about to ruin that, are you?"

I bit my lip and lowered my eyes. "'Ruin' is such an ugly word," I said. "I was just thinking that-"

"You don't love me anymore, is that it? You're tired of me? Or is there another girl?"

I had nothing to tell her except how I felt, and since I had already opened this can of worms there was no backing out, no way I could change my mind and tell her I was just kidding. Reluctantly, I told her the truth.

"Yeah. There is. Or, well, there could be. I mean, it's not like we're boyfriend and girlfriend or anything, not yet, but it looks like we might be headed in that direction. Believe me, Valerie, I didn't plan this. It just happened."

Tears began to form in her eyes, and I felt awful. I was breaking her heart, and there was absolutely no reason for it, except that . . . well . . . except that I had found someone I loved more, and . . . and, well, I don't know, Valerie, who can explain how we feel sometimes? I mean, when you love someone, you love 'em and there's not a whole lot you can do about it.

"But I love *you*," she pleaded. "And you love me."

"Well, yeah, I do. Or I did. I think. Anyway, people change. *I've* changed."

Valerie backed away from me a few steps, her demeanor changing again, this time from injured to suspicious. "What do you mean people change? I haven't changed. As of yesterday you hadn't changed. What happened? Who is this girl? I deserve to know that much, don't I?"

"Yes, you do," I said.

"Well? Who is she"

"Lisa McDooley."

"Lisa McDooley! *That* bimbo? Are you out of your mind?"

I could tell she wanted to laugh, but she was too shocked to do anything but stare at me as if I were an accident victim in the middle of the road.

"No, I'm not out of my mind. This is the real thing."

"I don't believe you."

"I know, I know. But I wanted to be fair and let you down as easily as possible."

"Easily? I'm in misery, and you think this is fair? When- when did you start dating her?"

"Well, we haven't actually gone out on a date yet."

"Have you kissed her?"

"Not yet, no."

"How long have you been together?"

"We're not actually together as a couple- yet -but it's only a matter of time. I wanted to be free for her when she's ready. She spoke to me yesterday, and the way she looked at me, well-"

"You're an idiot!"

"Look, I knew you weren't going to take this well, but if we can both just be mature about this-"

To her credit Valerie didn't sob, or slap me, or go hysterical that afternoon. Instead, she just looked at me with a bewildered, sad expression, and then brushed past me and headed back the way we had come.

I stood watching her walk down the shore and then up the path through the woods that led back to Shale Road and the lonely, winding walk home. I thought, *That wasn't as hard as I expected it to be. I guess breaking up is something girls learn to deal with.*

Something else girls learn to deal with, I found out later that week: girls, especially very beautiful popular girls like Lisa McDooley, also learn to deal with lovestruck fools who dump their girlfriends simply because they think that a friendly smile or a wink from the head cheerleader means she wants them and is open for business.

I spent the rest of that spring and most of that summer trying to win Valerie back, but she never came over to my house again, never returned my phone calls, and in fact didn't speak another word to me for over thirty years.

LESSON 19

Time Is On My Side

Repetition, repetition, repetition.
Strength.
Confirmation.

That was the mantra Coach Greenwood, the finest high school varsity football coach in east Tennessee in that fall season of 1971 and General Lee High School's dumbest history teacher.

"Repetition, boys," he'd say in his thick Junior Sample hillbilly accent, "repetition. If ya don't *re*-peat and *re*-peat and *re*-peat, how're ya gonna learn it?" Whatever "it" was didn't matter: whether we were learning about the War of 1812 or a new defensive scheme against the run, Coach Greenwood firmly believed that the only way to train young minds was to assume they had no more sense than a puppy learning not to pee on the azaleas: run the information past them, rote, a hundred and seventy-six times, give the choke collar a good jerk when you have to, and eventually they'll catch on. The parents nicknamed him "Borax" because they believed him to be the cleansing agent the neighborhood kids- America's youth -so badly needed.

Principal Wynne was so sensitive to our team's public image, and specifically to Coach Greenwood's ability to play mind games and turn young criminals into productive citizens, that he actively recruited players himself. Ricky Eagle and I were two of his projects.

Ricky's family and mine had moved together from New Jersey to Knoxville (more accurately, to Concord, which was about ten miles west on Kingston Pike) that summer, as the result of a shakeup at their company digs in New Jersey. In fact, the Eagles wound up living directly behind us, our houses separated by about a three acre tract of woods. How it happened that both houses wound up being for sale at the same time, in the same neighborhood and in the same price range, is one of those mysteries of serendipity that resists all attempts at rational explanation. Anyway, there we were, our two families completely out of our element: carpet baggers transplanted to the set of "Hee Haw." Like fools, Ricky and I had looked forward to the move.

One of the first things he and I did that summer, once our households were settled and more or less functioning within the parameters of local custom, was pitch in and buy a good portable radio in the hopes that maybe, on clear summer evenings we might be able to pick up the faint bouncing signal of WABC out of New York and hear the sadly familiar voices of Dan Ingram and Cousin Brucie calling out the Top 40 hits. Unfortunately, the best we were ever able to do was pull in a commercial-heavy singles station out of Nashville. It wasn't much, but it beat the twangy country crap glutting the airwaves in Knoxville. On those first hot July afternoons there wasn't much else to do anyway, so as a way to kill time, we lay back in the grass in front of a large field and listened to crappy country and bluegrass music, wishing we were someplace else.

The field we were fronting was at the dead end to a stretch of country road near our neighborhood, and from what we had heard, had gained quite a reputation as a favorite trolling spot for Sheriff Underwood to flush out teenage lovers and miscreants. To the kids it had become known simply as The Field.

Apparently, whoever owned the property hadn't used it for anything in years. There was speculation he might have even died or abandoned it. With very few places to hang out besides Jamie's 18-Hour Convenience Store or the quarry, the farm boys and the local jocks had more or less appropriated the field as a shooting range where they could shoot their .22s at soda bottles and the occasional rabbit, or blow the tops off of tree stumps with twelve gauges, and then come back at night and park under the stars with their giddy stupid girlfriends, trying to cop a feel and pull their pants down to their knees before Sheriff Underwood rolled up with his show-stopping search light and started taking names.

So there we were, Ricky and I, that sweltering July afternoon surrounded by warm summer vibes and taking in the cornball fascination of a world completely alien to us, when Ricky happened to look up and see a group of a dozen or so kids walking our way. "Wonder what they want," he said.

"They'd better not be looking for trouble," I said, "'cause you and I'll give it to 'em."

Now, in order to understand why I said this, you have to appreciate that the part of New Jersey Ricky and I were from was not exactly the ghetto, but it was in a part of the state where, whenever a cadre of teenagers is headed toward you it means only one of two things: either it's your own gang coming to pick you up, or it's some other gang coming to beat the life out of you. Either way, you've got to put up a front. You've got to come off tough, or else. We didn't know anyone in the neighborhood yet, and we assumed they were gunning for us, so we immediately shifted into badass mode.

Ready for a fight, Ricky clicked off the radio. This was a defining moment, but not exactly the way we were hoping to start our new life in Hicksville. These inbreds clamoring toward us didn't have any idea about the kind of wall they were about to run into. Ricky was 6' 4" and going into his senior year; I was smaller, but fearless as a wolverine. I knew how to fight and how to lie; I knew how to take pain and how to inflict it. I knew how to use people, but I didn't know the first thing about how to make friends.

Ricky stood up and faced the group coming down the street, his fists clenched at his sides. I stood too, tense but ready to put some hicks in traction if I had to. Yet, for the first time in my teenage life I was hoping I wouldn't have to fight.

A moment later the group passed us by without confrontation, without even stopping, with only a few cursory nods, some girlish, inside-joke giggles, one or two "hey"s- and little else. Like a tiny parade. As if we were an uninteresting zoo exhibit.

"What the-" Ricky's mouth hung open as the last of the group turned and cut into the open field and headed for the woods.

I let out a huge sigh of relief. "Yeah, what the-"

It was all very well, I realized then, to make a decision to change your view of things, but the truth was that our stance- with clenched fists, amped with attitude and anticipating raging bad times -fairly well represented who we were and what we had been taught over the years. This was who we had always been, who we were, and if things didn't change, who we would always be.

**

Later that summer, a week before school started, Ricky and I were up at the school tossing a football around on the field behind the athletic building. Like the high school itself, the athletic building had been built in 1912 out of hardwood and red brick and was a true throwback to a time when the world was informed with degrees of black and white, shaded with tones of sepia. A time when lunch pails under a shade tree and rulers across the knuckles were part of the school day.

"Take off," I told Ricky. "Wide triangle, strip 44, zebra go," I added, trying to sound like a real quarterback. Actually, it was the one football play I remembered from playing in a pickup game the previous fall with a couple of Rutgers third team rejects.

"Right!" Ricky said, and on a jet, he bolted down the field, cut into a post pattern, and headed for the goal line. I pulled the trigger, and with all the strength I had in me, lofted a pass forty yards downfield. At 6' 4", Eagle was an easy target.

"Touchdown!" he yelled.

"Whoo-hoo!"

A quick scamper down the field and we were high-fiving and throwing triumphant fists in the air. "These hayseeds don't nothin' about football," Ricky whooped. "They're gonna wish they had us on their team!"

"No such luck," I gloated. "What do we need with these donkeys?"

"Jest you 'member, fellers," came the voice of a short, stocky figure on the sideline. "A donkey kin kick yor ass through a stone wall." Where this guy had come from, we had no idea, but there he was, a talking potato wearing a General Lee High School coach's hat and spitting tobacco.

"You boys look like you mighta played this little game before," he added.

Ricky smiled cockily. "A time or two, yeah."

"Either of you ever played high school ball?" asked the coach.

Ricky and I looked at each other and laughed. "No."

The coach stared down at his shoes for a second and then raised his eyes to bore a hole between Ricky's eyes first, and then mine. "Ah'm Coach Greenwood," he said, extending his huge skillet-sized hand. "We could use some new blood on the team this season. And ah mean that in ever since of the word. You boys interested in bein' part of a winnin' team?"

Ricky blinked unbelievingly. "Yeah, sure; but we just told you we've never played on a team. What do we know?"

Coach Greenwood smiled as if he knew a secret he had no intention of telling a couple of cherries new to the school. "Don't worry about that. I need bodies. Ah'll teach you what you need to know."

Ricky and I looked at each other again; *how hard can it be?*

**

We discovered soon enough what the secret Coach Greenwood wasn't about to tell us was. Coach Greenwood had a reputation for being relentless in his discipline, uncompromising in his devotion to God and country, a **motivational genius who could get undersized, underweight football players to play inspired, totally destructive football against lunkheads who could bench press a small farm tractor and eat a whole pig at one sitting.** Coach Greenwood's artificial patriotism and prison style hollering were annoying, but Ricky and I had resigned ourselves to the fact that we were going to have to face that kind of mentality anywhere we went in the South anyway, so we took it in stride as much as we could. Besides, by the time school began, we had already committed ourselves to the team- Ricky as a wide receiver, me as a running back -and 6:30 a.m. practices.

"Repetition, repetition, repetition!

"Strength!

"Confirmation, gentlemen!"

Coach Greenwood must have yelled that mantra a dozen times a day. When our first game was still a week away, I wanted to quit; Ricky did too. I hated football, I hated practice. More than anything, I hated Coach Greenwood. Not as a person, but what he stood for, and how he presented the challenge of overwhelming competition to boys who- let's face it -were not nearly as worldly as they believed themselves to be. All I remembered from his interminable drills was, "Repetition, repetition, repetition!

"Strength!

"Confirmation, gentlemen!"

The General Lee Commodors were used to winning, *all the time*, in a community that expected them to win, *all the time*. That was doubly true when it came to our cross-town rival, the Limestone High School Bulldogs. That autumn, when Ricky Eagle and I blindly joined the team, ours was the number one ranked football team in the region. Not because of Ricky and me, of course- we were like two sprigs of parsley garnishing a steak dinner –but because Coach Greenwood had built a championship caliber squad around senior quarterback, Neil Close, who was not only the school board president's son, but as much as we all hated to admit it, was the driving force behind the team's success.

Even so, Neil wasn't Coach Greenwood's secret, and neither was his mantra of "Repetition!" It was only when I was at the Piggly Wiggly one Saturday afternoon on a grocery run for my mother that I learned his secret. I happened to be walking down the cereal aisle when I overheard Coach Greenwood's voice in the next aisle in the middle of a conversation with Hilda Close, Neil Close's mother.

"So, Coach," I heard Mrs. Close say, punctuating her speech with her renowned and disingenuous *I live in a ten thousand square foot custom home and I drive a top of the line Lincoln Continental, so you'd better tell me what I want to hear* tone, "how's the team looking? You've got a good, strong group behind my boy this year?"

I peaked around the aisle shelf and saw Coach Greenwood run his fingers through his thinning brown hair, a polite gesture really, a way of saying, *I knew you were going to ask me that.* He said, "Wish ah could tell ya, Mrs. Close. We got a lot of returning juniors, some strong seniors, plenty of beef up front. Got a coupla new boys on the team, too, from up north. We'll jest have to play the season and see."

The makeup on Mrs. Close's face cracked as she forced herself to smile. "Well, that certainly is . . . *reassuring*, Coach. As you know, we're all very proud of our team. I don't have to tell you how much we're all looking forward to the Commodores making roadkill out of the Bulldogs and the rest of the conference this season."

Coach Greenwood planted his feet firmly. "No, ma'am, you don't have to tell me. It's unnerstood," he said. "We got a lot of pride around here, don't we?"

Mrs. Close relaxed. "Oh, I am *so* relieved to hear you say that, Coach Greenwood. Yes, absolutely. There's the tradition to protect, and I just *know* you're the man who can do it. You always have." Then she clutched Coach by his elbow, flirtatiously. "I know we've got some tremendous players returning, my Neil included, of course."

"Of course."

"But I understand you say you've got some new boys as well this year? What kind of boys are they?"

Coach Greenwood got a twinkle in his dark brown eyes. "Ask me that question again in twenty years," he said.

"Twenty years?" Mrs. Close was obviously confused. "Why twenty years?"

"Because like all our kids, Mrs. Close, that's when we'll know what kind of men they turned out to be, what kinda husbands and fathers they turned out to be. They're on the edge of manhood. Let's give 'em time."

Well, as it turned out, we lost half our games that season, probably because Ricky and I joined the team, but we didn't mind. We had more fun that year than we had ever had in our lives.

And as it turned out, that was Coach Greenwood's secret: time.

LESSON 20

Playing Army

    Growing up in Somerville, I had practically lived in a Norman Rockwell painting. Our neighborhood had forty houses, each on its own odd-shaped acre, all of them lining Winding Creek Road and Rolling Hills Way. Winding Creek Road, my street, was a cul-de-sac, and Rolling Hills Way was a dead end that led right to the edge of the Willis farm, its upper and lower cow pastures lined with taut rust barbed wire fencing. All the houses were bounded in back by either woods, the makeshift baseball field, or the creek Winding Creek Road was named for. I remember my best friend C. J. and I used to spend hours damming up narrow sections of that creek in the summer and tramping along its icy surface in the winter to see where it led.

    A five minute walk from my mailbox led you across Pasture Lane, past the Zimmerman's barn, down narrow, winding Missionary Road, and past the old white steepled Methodist church. Another five minutes and you were lazing on the shady banks of the dark green Raritan River and a stone's throw from Martins' Market, the little mom and pop general store that had been in business since Woodrow Wilson took office.

    I remember lying in the cool dark shade of a summer afternoon and watching jets sail by high overhead, on their way to faraway places, and dreaming of someday being on one of those planes, bound for a land I had never seen- maybe never even heard of. I guess every boy fantasizes about adventures in foreign lands, about leaving home and coming back a hero. Maybe. Anyway, that was my summer dream.

So it should have come as no surprise that even after my family moved to Tennessee, at the first hint of Labor Day and the inevitable return to school, my mind still clung to those lazy daydreams of summer. I couldn't concentrate on my school work. Didn't want to. The teachers would drone on day after day . . .

Open the book and turn to page 182. James, would you read the first two paragraphs for us, please?

James would stumble his way through the passage, and I would nod off, my head bobbing.

Very good, James. Thank you. Linda, would you take the next two paragraphs, please?

Then Linda would start off strong, until she hit a three-syllable word and had a complete linguistic meltdown, and I knew that another session of my interminable public education had managed to stop time and plunge my imagination into complete darkness.

Year after year, from junior high school all the way through high school, it never got any better. Annoying homework, overbearing teachers, and dull, doltish classmates. I lost all interest in school, forgot any purpose I might have had in going. Before I realized what had happened I was a senior staring straight down the barrel of graduation and adulthood. Nothing waiting for me on the other side. No college plans. No work plans. No plans at all.

The 60s were a wild and unpredictable decade to be sure, but in our house there were two things that *were* predictable: the first was that my old man would down at least one martini before dinner. The other was that we always- *always* -watched the evening news on TV while we ate. Which meant that while I was soaking mom's meatloaf in ketchup, I got to watch soldiers soaking in blood in Vietnam. Huey's hovering over rice paddies, rows of dead Viet Cong regulars strewn along ditches, bandaged U.S. soldiers being 'coptered to safety under enemy fire. Vietnam was as much a part of dinner as a tall glass of milk.

Without paying much attention to what was happening, and with no one pointing out the hazard signs along the way, I coasted through high school oblivious to the damage I was doing to my academic record, numb to the horrors of Vietnam.

Until the last week in April.

I had been blithely, recklessly, careening toward graduation with as low a grade point average as it was possible to have and still be eligible for a diploma. But I wasn't too concerned; I didn't need to be. *Live for today; let tomorrow take care of itself* was the credo of the day, and I believed in it.

One night I was playing a game of chess with the old man in the den after a particularly satisfying steak dinner, and I had him on the defensive. Mom was finishing the dishes in the kitchen, my brother was picking his guitar in the next room, and life was good. Then, out of nowhere, the old man had me in check and said, "Mom tells me you got some mail today."

I studied the board. "Uh-huh. Got my Rolling Stone." I moved my knight's pawn forward two squares and blocked his attack.

"You got something from Washington, too, is that right?" the old man asked.

I looked up at him long enough to make *are-you-kidding-me?* eye contact, then returned my attention to the board as he advanced his rook's pawn one square. "Washington?" I said.

"Yep."

"Well, where is it?" It upset me that he or my mother would withhold mail intended for me. I wasn't sure, but I thought it might be a violation of my rights, or a federal law, or something.

"Your mother has it," he said. It was my move, but I had momentarily lost focus on the game and was more concerned with yet another in what seemed to be an endless series of invasions of my privacy.

"Hey, mom!" I called. "You got a letter for me? From Washington?"

She was a moment in responding, but finally she said, "yes," and walked into the den, wringing her hands on a dish towel. "It's over there on the table," she said, indicating the small antique table in the corner cluttered with framed photographs of family members.

I got up and walked over to the table to retrieve my mail. "Why didn't you give me this this afternoon?" I asked her, peeved. I stared down at the return address. *Department of Defense. Washington, D.C.* Addressed to *Mr. Clinton Heath Johnson III.*

"Because . . ." she stopped herself and shared a look with the old man.

The old man cleared his throat. "Because she knows what it is," he said.

"So?"

"So. It's not good."

"What do you mean it's not good? How in the world would you know? Did you open it and read it?" I knew they hadn't, but I was eighteen; I was worldly and knew everything. Parents were not to be trusted.

"Didn't have to," said the old man.

"Well, then, what is it?" I inserted my thumb under the sealed flap and ripped the envelope open along it's top fold.

"Your draft notice," my father said.

I pinched the letter inside with my fingers and pulled it out. A small stiff card came out with it. On one side, in a corner, the large black type was unmistakeable: **1-A**. I held in my hand something that, until that moment, I had only heard and read about: my draft card.

"Oh, God," I muttered. I sat back down on the edge of the sofa, across from the old man. "What do I do?"

"That's a great question," he said. "You don't have many options."

"Well, what options *do* I have?"

Mom had been standing there all the while, just listening. Now she came and sat beside me. "There's Conscientious Objector status," she said.

"What's that?" I asked.

"You apply to the government and tell them you can't go to war because you don't believe in it."

"That's it?" I said. "I can do that. I *don't* believe in war. It's idiotic."

The old man shook his head. "It's not that easy. You have to object on religious grounds. Even then, you're dealing with bureaucrats. The likelihood of you getting CO status is nil."

"I can fake it," I said. "I can be as religious as the next guy, if it means getting out of this."

My father looked pained. "You can try," he said, "but you'd better have a back-up plan ready."

"I can't- I don't *want* to go!" I protested.

"I know you don't," he said.

"What if I go to Mexico? Or Canada? I can go there 'til the war's over."

Mom rubbed my shoulders and pulled me close to her. "Sure, you can try that," my old man said. "But keep in mind, once you go, you can never come back."

"What about after the war's over?"

"Not legally," he said. "They can throw you in federal prison."

"Well then, what do I do?" I said, panic in my throat. "What do I do?"

"Honey?" my mom addressed the old man. "What about college? You can get a deferment if you're in college, can't you?"

The old man gave it a few seconds of thought. "Well, sure. You can usually defer if you're in school. But with Heath's grades . . ."

And that was when it hit me for the first time: *grades*. No one had ever attached any significance to them, never told me *why* I needed good grades. Oh sure, the counselors had mentioned the importance of earning high grades in order to "get into the college of your choice," but they were talking about jobs, careers. What seventeen-year-old is seriously thinking about a career? That's not where *my* head was. That's not where anybody's head was that I knew of. College and a career were a lifetime away; Vietnam was on the other side of the world. None of any of this had anything to do with me.

I lowered my eyes to the chessboard, and trembled. The Army. Vietnam. Just stuff on TV at dinnertime. College. Nothing anybody at home or at school had prepared me for. Not in the way they should have. Not in the way I needed.

Life Lessons 101

For maybe the first time in my life I understood the enormous leap you made from teenager to adulthood when you graduated high school. Leave it to the army to finally get the point across. Between the warm, automatic insulation of my life at home with mom and the old man, and the cold, hungry, dangerous reality of the world outside, a deep dark hole no one ever told me about threatened to swallow up my future, my whole life.

As it happened, shortly after I received my draft notice, the Selective Service Board switched to a lottery system based upon eligible recruits' birthdays, and my birth date never came up before the last of the American troops withdrew from Saigon in 1975. I took the S.A.T. college entrance exam and through exceptional genes or dumb luck, or both, scored high enough on the test to qualify for acceptance into the Humanities program at Boston University, an invitation I jumped at with the obnoxious, crazy energy of a religious convert. Of course, once I got there, I discovered just how much intellectual ground I had to make up because of my slovenly slacker ways in high school, but this time school was a bull I was more than prepared to ride.

LESSON 21

INCHOATE VICISSITUDES

After screwing around so much in high school, and a year working minimum wage jobs, I had a great deal of intellectual ground to make up when I finally managed to fool the dean of admissions at Boston University to open up a desk for me at that august institution. Sitting in my first humanities class at B. U. (a.k.a. "Big and Ugly") in the fall of 1974, I realized just how far behind I was as my instructor and a roomful of smartass seventeen and eighteen-year-olds sat in a wide "critique and commentary circle" with their legs crossed, smoking cigarettes and pontificating about the existentialist nature of the post-Edwardian prose of some obscure nineteenth century English writer whose dusty books I had never read nor even heard of.

It was humbling, to say the least. The reasons I had paid so little attention to my studies in high school were many and varied, but suffice to say they revolved primarily around the double helix center of my world at the time, my girlfriend Valerie and an arrogant belief that my teachers and classmates were nincompoops- which they may very well have been -but it doesn't do you much good to go around thinking that way when you're a teenager with no world experience.

Anyway, I arrived in the world of higher education with a raw talent for academic achievement, but absolutely no practical experience. I was academically overmatched and intimidated at every turn. Not only that, I was homesick. I missed trees. Except along the Charles River, Boston doesn't have many trees, or at least, it didn't have many along Commonwealth Avenue when I was there. I had grown up in north central New Jersey and east Tennessee, and I had come to Boston by way of east Texas, so all the concrete was a bit overwhelming for an under-sophisticated nineteen-year-old. So in the summer of 1975 I transferred to the University of Tennessee at Knoxville, back to more familiar territory.

With a whole new attitude toward learning for learning's sake, and grateful for a second chance to twist my head on properly, I devoted my sophomore year at U.T. Knoxville to good pizza, looking for a pair of arms to fall into, and filling my brain with as much information as I could. But I didn't just want information, I wanted knowledge; I wanted to actually *know* things and to be able to discuss them intelligently with other people. I wanted to learn how to think and to apply what I knew. I'm happy to report that by the autumn of my junior year I had not only managed to make up all the lost academic ground, but I had pulled far enough ahead to have forged some fairly significant bonds in the elite and academic social club that is university life on the hill.

One of the more peculiar individuals I met that fall was Samuel Fogarty. I say he was peculiar, but I mean that in a complimentary way. Samuel was not athletic, nor was he a lady's man. He thought rock and roll in general, and the Beatles specifically, was the most insipid form of so-called music since hillbillies first strung catgut across a box fiddle. He detested Hollywood and all that it stood for, and his general opinion of humanity was that the overwhelming majority of the world's population could be categorized as unhealthily ignorant and bereft of logic, doomed to intellectual poverty. Because of this, the world's future was in a constant state of moral, ethical, and cerebral peril. Let's face it: he was a right wing snoot.

Samuel was also alarmingly brilliant. Besides being a voracious reader with a photographic memory who could put away two or three full-length books a day and recount the details of each with jaw-dropping accuracy, he was also a classically trained virtuoso on the piano. Chopin was his favorite, though he had a wide range of musical heroes. At twenty-three, he was finishing his dissertation for his doctorate in education.

I had worked very hard indeed to get to the top of the ant mound where professors' assistants, graduate students, associate professors, and brown-nosers hung out, but I could never quite understand what Samuel saw in me that caused him to deem me worthy of private conversation with him, and to actually be my friend. My hunch was that he saw me as some kind of lab rat, someone he could try out his educational and psychological theories on, but there were times when I wondered if his interest in me as a friend was genuine. You can never tell with those kinds of egg heads. No matter. We spent time together and discussed the problems of the world until they were solved.

Because the dorms didn't serve dinner on Sunday nights, Samuel and I would go out to eat around seven o'clock, usually at Floppy's Burgers, a favorite grease spot of mine. I couldn't help it, I loved their spicy curly fries. Again, I'm not sure why Samuel readily agreed to eat at a place so far beneath his otherwise highbrow tastes, but he always seemed to have a good time, and our conversations lasted hours, so what did it matter?

One Sunday night Samuel and I were sitting at our regular booth in Floppy's, talking about the current educational model and its roots in the Industrial Revolution of the nineteenth century, when Samuel, having just finished making an astute observation, grinned with conceit. Obviously satisfied that what he had just put out in the space between us was over my head, he sat back in the booth and dabbed the corners of his mouth with a paper napkin. Then, after folding the napkin neatly, he interlaced his fingers behind his head and sighed, "Ah, yes. The vicissitudes of life!"

Vicissitudes? I thought. *What the heck are vicissitudes? What's he talking about?*

It had happened again. Ignorance had caught me by the throat and shaken me in its clenched, rabid jaws. How could I not know what vicissitudes meant? Well, naturally, I didn't want to appear ignorant- I had worked far too hard and soared far too high into the restricted airspace Samuel Fogarty and his ilk occupied to stall out and plunge into an intellectual nosedive simply because I didn't know what a dumb word meant -so I nodded my head in feigned, snobbish agreement. Yes indeed. Vicissitudes.

"I know just what you mean," I said.

Samuel pinched an especially long curly fry between his thumb and forefinger and ate it slowly, all the while studying me with that self-congratulatory smirk that would crawl across his face whenever he knew he had a lab rat like me cornered. With a bit of clumsy wordplay I tried to pass off as erudition, I managed to change the subject to the disappointing season the basketball team was having, and how they were breaking every true big orange Volunteer sports fan's heart, thus steering our conversational ship into a much shallower and safer harbor.

We finished our burgers and fries and headed back to the dorms, but as we walked across the campus discussing more mundane subjects- our schedules for the week, the recent spate of bad movies they had been showing at the Student Center, the theater department's new production -I couldn't seem to shed the unseen and unspoken embarrassment of not having known what vicissitudes meant. My shame was nearly palpable; Daniel Webster's ghost might as well have been walking between us wagging a translucent finger in my face. In fact, I think he was.

Vicissitudes. Vicissitudes. What does it mean?

I was obsessed. I had to know. No way Samuel Fogarty was going to go the whole week believing he had verified yet another theory about his little lab rat. The next time I saw him I was going to know what vicissitudes meant. No- better! I was going to use it in a sentence! I was going to work it into our next conversation somehow!

When I returned to my dorm room and saw my roommate Steve sitting forlornly on his bed with his microbiology book spread across his lap and a vacant stare on his face, I knew he had run into a similar wall that evening, though his was emotional, not intellectual. He kept mumbling the name of his ex-girlfriend over and over. "Jane. Jane. Oh, Jane."

"Oh, oh," I said. "Did you call Jane again?"

Steve sighed heavily.

"I've told you not to do that, I said. No good ever comes from calling Jane, you know that."

He sighed heavily again.

"Steve," I said, with unintentional urgency in my voice and attempting to rescue him from the dangerous shoals of unrequited love, "have you ever heard the word 'vicissitudes'?"

With a wan, pathetic expression, he turned his eyes toward me and sighed a third time. "No."

"Are you sure?" I said. "'Vicissitudes,' as in 'the vicissitudes of life.'"

"No, never heard of it," he said with an irritated squint, and sighed heavily again.

"Yeah, me either," I said. I searched the pile of papers and books on my desk and found my beaten and lopsided 3rd Edition College Dictionary. "Vicissitudes, vicissitudes," I mumbled, flipping the pages frantically. "V-I-S, V-I-S-S, V-I-S-C, V-I-C . . . Ah! Here it is! 'Vicissitudes: A change of fortune or circumstances, typically one that is unwelcome or unpleasant.' Well, that'd be me right now. Vicissitudes. Vicissitudes. I've gotta remember that. Vicissitudes. Like the vicissitudes of your relationship with Jane."

Steve turned his vacant, beady eyes on me. "Huh?"

"Call her again," I deadpanned.

The following Sunday Samuel and I met at Floppy's for our usual artery-plugging dinner and soon enough our conversation was underway, only this time I was armed and ready. All I needed was an opening, anything remotely having to do with the ups and downs of life, and I was going to launch "vicissitudes" into the heart of our discourse and show Samuel K. Fogarty that he wasn't the only educated man sitting in that booth.

At last, it came: my opportunity to return fire and shoot the best word I had ever learned back into the belly of the beast. "Well, you know, Samuel, if you take into account the vicissitudes of middle class life in hard economic times," I said, "I'm sure you'll agree they have little recourse but to endure."

"Perhaps," he mused. "But on the whole, given the inherent instability of middle class spending habits, I'm not sure your inchoate hypothesis can stand."

My what *hypothesis?* Inchoate? *What the heck's* inchoate?

He had done it to me again! This time, though, I had an edge: a pocket dictionary. When he got up to go refill his Coke, I quickly pulled out my paperback Webster's and, keeping one eye on Samuel and one eye on the dictionary in my lap under the table, looked up "inchoate." When he returned to the booth I secreted the book back into the waistband of my jeans and stroked my chin thoughtfully.

Samuel sat down and took a long, conceited sip of his Coke. I ate a clump of curly fries and washed it down with a sip of root beer. "You know," I said, "now that I think about it, my idea may be a little inchoate after all. Still, I've been thinking about it a long time, and I think it has a future."

Samuel grinned that maddening grin again and slurped at his Coke with an emperor's abandon. "Yes," he said at last, "maybe it does."

Later that night, after he and I had gone our separate ways, I broke out my little dictionary again, looked up *inchoate*, and felt like an idiot. It was then that I started to catch on: you don't learn something and then close the book. The book is always open, and the learning never ends.

ABOUT THE AUTHOR

Heath Johnson was born in Illinois and grew up in New Jersey and Tennessee. A graduate of the University of Tennessee, Knoxville, he is the author of five completed novels, as well as a collection of short stories and a novella of the most popular story with his students, *"Jellybeans."*

He has backpacked and ridden motorcycles all across the United States, especially across the Southwest, is an avid reader, long distance bicycler, and listens to music constantly.

He lives in Texas with his wife and two teenage sons.

Made in the USA
Lexington, KY
14 May 2014